THE VIRGIN
MONEY
MAKER

THE VIRGIN

MONEY

MAKER

CHRIS NEWLANDS

BORROW IT, SAVE IT, INVEST IT . . . BETTER!

I'd like to thank Carl Bridge, Carolyn Thorne and Gareth Fletcher
for all their help in putting this book together. I'd also like to thank
all those people who gave up their time to contribute to the case
studies and expert views used within this book. Finally, I'd like to use
this opportunity to tell my mum, my dad, my two sisters and Lydia
that I love them very much.

First published in Great Britain in 2007 by
Virgin Books Ltd
Thames Wharf Studios
Rainville Road
London
W6 9HA

A catalogue record for this book is available from the British Library.

ISBN 978 0 7535 1207 4

The paper used in this book is a natural, recyclable product made from wood grown
in sustainable forests. The manufacturing process conforms to the regulations of the
country of origin.

Designed by Virgin Books Ltd

Printed and bound in Germany by APPL

CONTENTS

Introduction

'Hi, it's Andrew Dylan-Jones. Message for Clive, can you tell him to call his IFA ASAP, it's about a UK equity ISA. Ciao.'

Mean anything to you? Probably not, but that's a message I once took for a mate at work who – like you – was innocently trying to sort out his finances. You won't be surprised to find out that Clive never returned Dylan-Jones's call. In fact, he didn't answer his work phone for a week. Dylan-Jones, who I suspect wasn't Italian, had scared the life out of Clive.

Now, before I go on I want to assure you of three things: one, Dylan-Jones was a pillock; two, you'll know exactly what he was on about by the time you finish this book; and three, you're big enough, old enough and certainly clever enough to get your head around any jargon the Dylan-Joneses of this world may throw at you.

The truth is, sorting out your finances is easy. You want your debts to be as cheap as possible, your savings to return the highest level of interest available and your investments to return you a healthy pot of cash over the long term. Simple. But whether you've got more money than a footballer's wife or are one of the many people contributing to the UK's debt mountain – a mountain that is growing by £1 million every four minutes – you could probably do with a bit of help. Not least because you're up against an industry ready to throw acronyms – such as ISA, APR, AER, PPI and HLC – in your eyes, watch you stagger around blindly and then spike whatever it is you're buying with so many hidden fees and charges you'll think your last name is Milligan.

But don't let that put you off. With a little bit of guidance you can save a packet on your debts, take home a tidy sum from your savings and make some serious money from your investments. To do that, however, you have to learn a couple of new tricks – the most important of which is to shop around. Sadly, most of us use the same Fat Belly bank we joined as kids for all our financial needs. Remarkably, in return for just a few ceramic pigs and a black holdall, the Chubby banks seem to have bought our unswerving loyalty. The time has come, however, to be unfaithful.

Staying loyal to one provider might seem like an easy option, but it also means you're probably paying 20% interest on your credit card debts when you could be paying zero; that your money is stashed away in a current account that offers 60 times less interest than what you could be earning elsewhere; and that you've secured yourself just two chances of investing in the best long-term funds – fat chance and no chance.

The trick to being a Money Maker is to keep your options open. You'd never buy a digital camera, laptop or flat-screen TV unless you'd shopped around for the best deal first, so why wouldn't you do the same with a personal loan, a savings account or a long-term equity fund? If your credit card isn't the cheapest on the market, get rid of it. If your current account isn't offering the market's highest rate of interest, cut it loose. And if your investments are being stifled by unnecessarily high fees, it's time to kick them to the kerb.

A three-year £10,000 personal loan with an online provider could save you £60 a month compared to one peddled by a high-street bank, while buying a £200,000 home with a mortgage rate just one percentage point lower than the one you've got could save you 2,000 quid a year.

Making these sorts of savings is not difficult. In fact, most of what'll be thrown at you is, in essence, very straightforward; it's just it'll be littered with mumbo jumbo. Financial providers love nothing more than a confused customer – it makes you more susceptible to their sales pitch – but this book will help you to cut through the gobbledegook and get your finances back on track.

I can't promise it'll rid you of Dylan-Jones, but it will enable you to deal with him better, cut out the impractical and concentrate on the achievable – being a Money Maker.

Ciao.

PART 1:
BORROW
IT

Dropping and swapping

If there's one thing to remember when it comes to borrowing, it's that it pays to be promiscuous. The sad fact is that you are more likely to change your partner than you are your bank, but, in order to prosper when it comes to your debts, you must teach yourself to drop and swap.

To win, you have to be comfortable jumping shamelessly among credit card companies, feel at ease switching from one loan supplier to the next and feel content moving among different mortgage providers. Fail to do that and you risk waking up 25 years down the line bitter, out of pocket and wondering how the relationship began in the first place.

The fact is that every one of us (assuming you are all over the age of eighteen, and, if you're not, put the book down and get back to school) is almost £27,000 in debt. The bulk of our borrowing is made up of a mortgage, but more than £4,500 is via credit cards, motor and retail finance deals, overdrafts and unsecured personal loans.

The problem is that, while I have friends who will walk an extra ten minutes out of their way to save 15p on a pint of milk, those same friends – let's call them you – will apply for the first credit card, mortgage or loan deal to come through the letterbox at a cost of several hundred pounds a year. (It is estimated that banks and finance institutions send more than 1 billion flyers through the post each year.)

Had you spent the extra ten minutes it took you to walk down the high street to the cheap-pint-of-milk shop surfing the Internet or scouring the national newspapers for the cheapest credit-card, mortgage or loan deals, you could have saved enough money to buy hundreds of pints of milk, a cow and maybe even a maid to milk it for you.

But *noooooooooooo*! You are programmed to think you cannot actually save money when it comes to your debts. You cut out coupons, collect vouchers, ask for discounts, buy in bulk and walk ten minutes out of your way to save money on consumer goods – but will put up with higher rates and costly fees on your debts until that cow we just spoke about comes home.

The key is to treat credit in the way you would any other purchase. That may not require you to cut out coupons or buy in bulk, but it may involve you walking that extra ten minutes and will almost certainly require you to get online and flick through the national newspapers. All of these sources, such as www.moneysavingexpert.com, www.thisismoney.com, www.fool.co.uk, *FT Weekend* and the *Sunday Telegraph*, provide a wealth of information on the cheapest and best forms of debt and could end up saving you a heap of money.

All too often we use the same bank we have been using since we were kids (don't even try to tell me you weren't collecting one of those pigs) for all our borrowing needs. This concept works well in some areas – for example, when it comes to food shopping and you want to go to one place for everything you need – but for borrowing it's a mistake. A supermarket will offer you twenty different brands of toothpaste, ten different kinds of olive oil and five different types of baked beans. There are two chances that your bank will offer you such variety: fat chance and no chance.

To save money you need to kick the habit of using one provider. According to a survey by the high-street bank Abbey, almost 50% of us stay with the same provider because we believe all banks are the same, while almost a quarter of us stay with the same Fat Belly bank because we believe a new provider will not offer better facilities. Rubbish!

Get a £10,000 loan out over three years with a high-street bank instead of an online provider and you could end up paying an extra £60 a month. Rack up debts of £5,000 on a credit card issued by your local bank instead of one you've found at the top of a best-buy table and it could cost you a further £800 a year. And, more alarmingly, go for a mortgage rate just one percentage point higher than the current cheapest rate on the average price of a house (almost £180,000) and you'll be hit for an extra £32,500 over the course of 25 years.

Shop around. The Office of Fair Trading (OFT) found that almost a third of us arranged credit with one provider without first comparing that deal with any other. Don't. The OFT is so worried about this it has issued some key questions we should ask before signing up to any credit:

- **How much will it cost you compared with similar deals?**
- **Is it the best interest rate you can get?**
- **Will the interest stay the same?**
- **What do you have to pay each month and for how long?**
- **What is the total amount you will pay back?**
- **What happens if you miss a payment?**
- **Are there any extra charges if you repay the debt early?**

'By asking our key questions, people will be able to make a more informed decision on what credit deal best suits them,' says the OFT's chairman. 'Credit is not an add-on to a major purchase: it is a major purchase on its own – and a wrong decision can lead to long-term grief.' Well said, Mr Chairman.

Opening a credit card, applying for a loan and arranging a mortgage are as important as buying a computer, a car or a fancy TV. Admit it, if you were buying a laptop you would ask your mates if they had any tips, buy a computer magazine to find out which one it rated the most or go online to get some advice. The same principles need to be applied when it comes to your debts.

More than five thousand people a day seek professional advice about their debts and so there is no need to feel embarrassed asking your friends if they know who the best loan, credit or mortgage firms are. The odds are they will have recently shopped around for such deals themselves. But, if you do find it uncomfortable talking about borrowing, then the Internet is the perfect place for you. Log on to a few price-comparison sites. Good ones include www.uswitch.com, www.moneysavingexpert.com, www.moneyfacts.co.uk and www.fool.co.uk. Pick out the cheapest rates from a number of listed best-buy tables.

These tables – which are also found in every quality Sunday paper – cut out all the hard work of comparing deals. You will find league tables on every form of borrowing, be it credit cards, overdrafts or mortgages. In very simple terms, the deals found at the top of each table are the best, and, unless they're the ones you're already using, they're the ones you should think about investigating.

Forget the idea of being loyal to your existing provider. If they offer you the cheapest rates and the best service, fine, stay loyal. But, if they're taking you for granted, offering you extortionate rates and banking on the fact that you are expected never to leave, then it's time to prove them wrong.

Misplaced loyalty could cost you hundreds of pounds a year. Your Fat Belly bank will not think twice about charging you up to £40 if you go beyond your overdraft limit, while your credit-card firm will readily fine you for exceeding your credit limit and sting you for up to a fiver just for taking money out of the wall. Worse still, repay your mortgage late just once in 25 years and you're likely to be slapped in the face with a fine.

Your loyalty is wasted on these Chubby banks. And, if you're feeling cheated or short-changed by your provider, it's time to flail your arms, cause a scene and leave.

An eye for detail

Although the best-buy tables are a great and easy tool to use for working out which firms are offering the most attractive overdraft, mortgage or credit-card deals, make sure you always read the small print. Getting to the top of one of these tables is very lucrative for the Fat Belly banks. They know savvy consumers like yourselves use them to search for the most eye-catching offers and will often play around with their deals to get your attention. For example, one mortgage rate may be substantially cheaper than another but upon closer inspection you might discover it also carries an enormous arrangement fee. Likewise one credit card rate may look much better than the rest but may jump up to extortionate levels after only a few months. Be alert. More often than not, a rate you'll find in a best-buy table is far superior to the one you're using, but you need to be wise to any catches and make sure you know exactly what you're getting yourself into.

Don't scratch your credit record

Crucial to your ability to drop and swap and to be able to move provider if the rates it offers get progressively worse is the health of your credit record. Your capacity to jump ship and take advantage of the cheapest mortgage rates and the most eye-catching credit-card deals depends on how attractive you are to loan providers. I'm not talking about how much gel you put in your hair or how flat your stomach is. It's about your financial standing.

Companies will not give you a three-year loan or a 25-year mortgage if they think they'll never see the money again. It's as simple as that. If, on the other hand, you are seen as a safe bet, providers will jump over themselves to extend you credit.

Key to all of this is your credit score, probably one of the most important pieces of information in your financial life. It is based on a range of information about your financial past. It takes into account how you have handled debt previously and how much debt you have now.

Credit-reference agencies have details of all the credit cards and loans you have taken out and what repayments you have made. They are also aware of any late or missed payments, County Court judgments and bankruptcy filings – and also know of any instances when you may have applied for credit and been refused. Fart in a crowded room and I'm sure they'd know it was you.

Providers use the information credit-reference agencies compile about you, together with other details, such as your salary and employment details, to work out whether they'll extend you any credit.

A poor credit rating, which could be due simply to you not having a landline, signing up for lots of credit cards within a short space of time or living in an undesirable area, hinders your chances of getting a mortgage, loan or credit card and can also result in you being offered lower credit limits or less attractive interest rates.

The golden rule is never to miss repayments on your existing debts. Even if you just pay the minimum amount due each month (but try not to) it will bolster your credit score. Also, make sure you are registered on your local electoral roll, since this is used to verify your address.

It is also true that if you have never had any debt or used credit before your rating will not be as strong as that of someone who has taken out debt and kept up repayments – a blank credit report is no guarantee to a lender that you will be a good customer. To build up a positive rating, it may be worth opening a higher-interest-rate credit card, which is easier to do than for a lower-rate card. Use it sparingly and ensure you pay the full balance back each month.

Also get into the habit of checking your credit file, since you may have unknowingly become a victim of identity theft. Not that someone is running around with a false moustache and a wig pretending to be you but that someone might have acquired your personal financial information to apply for credit in your name.

Callcredit, Experian and Equifax, three of the UK's leading credit-reference agencies, will allow you access to your credit report for a small fee (£2 for a copy through the post) and can also – for a charge – alert you by text if there is any significant change to your report.

If your credit record is not in great shape, key to repairing it is to settle your bad debts as soon as you can and meet payments on existing loans. Unpaid credit and County Court judgments will stay on your file for six years, but they will be marked as settled once you pay them. Lenders will also allow you to write a statement to balance out a bad report, which could explain circumstances that might have tarnished your rating. There is no quick fix, however, but, if you settle bad debts and meet current payments on time, your score should improve within five years.

Nine ways to dirty your credit file

1. Not being registered on the electoral roll or not staying on it for long enough.
2. Reapplying for a loan straight after you have been refused one.
3. Moving home a lot.
4. Living abroad.
5. Renting a flat.
6. Becoming a victim of identity fraud.
7. Signing up for lots of credit cards within a short space of time.
8. Not paying your yearly car tax to the Driver and Vehicle Licensing Agency on time.
9. Not having a landline

Setting the record straight: gobbledegook about credit scores

- **Previous occupants of your house or flat influence your credit health.** Rubbish. Lenders carry out checks on people, not addresses. When you apply for credit Mr Provider will see information only on you and anyone you are financially tied to, for example the person you have a joint mortgage with.

- **You can pay to have adverse information removed from your credit file.** Tosh. Information can be removed or altered only if it is wrong and the credit-reference firm, whether it is Callcredit, Experian or Equifax – the three main agencies – will do this for free if it turns out to be the case. Stay clear of self-professed credit-repair firms, which claim to be able to clean up your credit profile – they can't.

- **Credit-reference companies operate blacklists.** Nonsense. The information credit-reference agencies hold is purely factual. It shows only whether or not you have managed your credit payments well. There is no such thing as a credit blacklist and no list of people who should be avoided at all costs.

- **Your credit report shows when you have been turned down for credit.** Hot air. What is recorded is that a lender – with your permission – took a peek at your information when you applied for a loan of some sort. This is known as a footprint and shows the date that the credit check took place, the type of credit you applied for and the name of the organisation you applied to. It does not show whether your application was refused or granted. Having a lot of these footprints on your file

during a short space of time, however, is a cause for concern for credit providers.

● **Negative information listed about you affects the rest of your household.** Claptrap. Unless you have joint finances with someone, such as a joint mortgage with your husband, wife, boyfriend or girlfriend, your credit history does not affect them and their credit history does not affect you. Lenders are not able to see information about you when someone you live with applies for credit or vice versa.

Casebook: Broken record – my story

I was in a department store about to pay for a pair of jeans when the sales assistant asked if I wanted to open a store card and that I would save 15% on the jeans if I did so. The upshot was that after spending ten minutes filling out the application form (my plan was to get the discount, pay off the amount and cut up the card) I was embarrassingly told my application had been declined. I put back the jeans and walked out.

But I couldn't understand why. I had an overdraft with my bank and was paying off my student loans but I had never missed any payments and never took my overdraft beyond the agreed limit. I wrote off to one of the big credit-reference agencies to ask them to send me a copy of my file, which cost me £2, only to find that I had apparently defaulted on a payment of £106 to a mail-order catalogue company I had never heard of or bought anything from.

The debt was listed against a flat with a communal letterbox

I had been living in while I was a student but, according to my credit report, the item had been ordered more than a year after I had moved out.

The contact details of the mail-order company were listed on the credit file and I contacted them immediately to tell them what had happened. I explained that I had not been living at the address when the item had been bought and that it was not I who made the purchase. I was told to put everything down in a letter along with proof that I was living somewhere else at the time.

I wrote the letter, adding copies of bills I had paid at my new address. The mail-order company agreed I had been a victim of fraud, amended their own records and contacted the credit-reference agency to inform them. My file was corrected seven days later.

A few months later I was able to apply successfully for a credit card and these days I tend to check my credit file every eighteen months to make sure it hasn't happened again. I may be a bit paranoid but I wanted to buy a flat and get a mortgage and I didn't want anything to jeopardise that.

A quick word of warning on borrowing

Never get into more debt than you can afford to pay off. By all means shop around for the cheapest deals but do not apply for loans or rack up expenses on credit cards unless you have enough money to meet those payments. Borrowing is great because it allows you to spread the cost of an expensive item across a period of several months, and from time to time we all need to do that. But do not borrow for the sake of it. Dropping and swapping is about saving money on existing and carefully considered debts – not about applying for an unmanageable level of debt.

One person becomes a victim of insolvency every minute of the working day. Don't become one of them. If you are having problems with debt, it's never too late to do something about it. Contact one of the free, independent debt-counselling charities, such as the Consumer Credit Counselling Service (0800 138 1111) or National Debtline (0808 808 4000), or talk about it with someone you can trust. As a starting point, these five steps put together by the Citizens Advice Bureau should help you:

● Make a complete list of your debts and remember to divide them into separate headings – priority and nonpriority debts. You will have to make offers to pay off your priority debts before you tackle your nonpriority debts.

● Work out your income and expenditure. Be honest and make sure that the amounts are realistic. Your resulting budget will show you whether you have any money left over to divide up among those you owe money. You may even be able to identify where you can make some savings. If you encounter problems, an advice agency can give you confidential help.

● Do not ignore creditors' letters or phone calls. Contact your creditors as early as possible and explain why you are in debt. If you phone, follow up the call with a letter, confirming what you said on the phone. Send the creditors a copy of your budget and list of your debts. If you do not feel confident to deal with your creditors, contact a free advice agency.

● If you have only a small amount of money available for your creditors after your essential spending, you may have to offer all of this to your priority creditors. You could have very little, or nothing, to offer to nonpriority creditors and you should explain this to them.

● Do not borrow more money to repay your debts. Think about the ways in which you might earn extra money or increase your income instead. If your income is low, you may be able to claim benefits.

Credit cards: shop 'til you drop

Shop 'til you drop? Credit cards? Wait a minute – that's what got me into this mess in the first place, you might be thinking. But it's not a plastic-fuelled trolley dash up and down your local high street I'm prescribing. Shopping around for the cheapest credit-card deal is what this is all about.

But, just to prove to you how much money you could save by chucking away your pricey bit of plastic and swapping it for a cheaper one, I'm going to have to assume you are Mr or Ms Average – sorry. As well as meaning you earn roughly £25,000 a year, will live to 75 and spend 26 hours a week in front of the TV, it also means you owe £4,580[1] on your existing credit card and pay 16.5% in annual interest.

Those mathematicians among you will have already worked out the dent that puts in your finances but for those not so at ease with numbers I have put my very own maths GCSE, a scrap of paper and a pencil to good use: it's costing you £733 a year to keep that shiny little sucker in your purse or wallet. Money you could use to buy another 74 copies of this book, 733 items from your local pound shop or 325 pints of beer.

Now imagine you're not so Mr or Ms Average and your particular card carries an interest rate of 20% (it shouldn't be too difficult – some carry charges of up to 29%). Well, now it's costing you £916 every twelve months. And if you've racked up debts of £10,000 instead of £4,580? You can make that £2,000. For the record, a debt of £10,000 at a rate of 29% would set you back £2,900 a year – and that's a lot of beer.

---

1 Includes retail finance deals, overdrafts and unsecured personal loans.

At this point you've got two options. The first is to lift up that average mattress of yours to expose the £4,580 you've been hiding for just such occasions. The second – and I'm guessing more likely alternative – is to trade in your credit card for a cheaper one. Thankfully, there are many such cards on the market.

But where do I find them?

Assuming it's Sunday (and there is a 14.2% chance it will be), your best bet is to run down to your local newsagent and pick up any one of the quality papers on sale. Housed within the personal-finance pages of your chosen paper – for example you can find the *Observer*'s eight-page personal-finance supplement within its business pages – you will find a number of best-buy tables that look a little something like this:

Card	BT Rate	BT Period	Typical APR
Fat Belly bank	0%	9 mths	15.9%
Chubby bank	0%	9 mths	15.9%
Big-Boned bank	0%	7 mths	14.9%

Don't worry: you are more than capable of getting your head round a table like this. The first thing to remember about these best-buy tables – which are also posted all over the Internet and found in numerous personal-finance magazines – is that someone has already done the work for you. That simply means that the card at the top of the table is the best and, unless it happens to be the one tucked away in your purse or wallet, it's the one you should consider getting.

But what is the BT rate?

That is the balance-transfer rate or the initial rate of interest the new provider will charge you once you've switched your average debt of £4,580. For all the banks in the table you can see that this is equal to zero. Before you start dishing out 'high fives', however, you need to be aware that these introductory rates do not last for ever.

Is that where the BT period comes in?

Yep. See? You're getting the hang of this. The BT period or balance-transfer period is how long the introductory period lasts. For Fat Belly bank's card you can see that this is nine months, while for the Big-Boned bank's card the BT period is set at seven months. At the end of this period you then have to pay the firm's much higher non-introductory rate or typical APR. By the way, APR is not short for April – it is the annual percentage rate or the cost of your credit card as a yearly measure.

Cue your newfound promiscuity

All that's left now is for you to practise your rate-hunting skills. Revel in your 0% rate and move on before it runs out. Do, however, *remember* to move on. A credit-card company would love nothing more than for you to forget when your introductory period expires. Don't.

You have to pay interest charges at a standard rate for only two months in order to lose all the benefits of a six-month interest-free period, or equally shell out standard-rate charges for three months to nullify nine months of 0% rates. Even if you switch card companies one day after your free period expires, you will be hit for a whole month's worth of interest.

The trick is to be alert. Put an X in your calendar, set your mobile phone to ring in nine months' time or tie a knot in something special. Failing that, sign up to www.moneysavingexpert.com's 'tart alert', a free text or email service that lets you know six weeks before your introductory period is about to finish that a big fat rate is waiting to say hello.

If you decide to stay with your card provider because you like the loyalty points they offer, such as air miles or Nectar points, or because you prefer their call centre being in Newcastle rather than

New Delhi, fine – you should stay put. But, if paying the lowest rate is all that matters to you – and according to Virgin Money that includes 74% of you – then run, Forrest, run.

Credit cards – in numbers

There are more credits cards in circulation than there are people in the UK with nearly 300 plastic transactions and 86 withdrawals taking place every second. We each owe more than £4,500 in credit-card debt with one in sixteen of us racking up non-mortgage debts larger than our wages. Three and a half million of us regularly only ever make the minimum repayments on our bit of plastic with almost one in ten credit-card balances at least three months in arrears. Paying the minimum monthly repayment of 2% on a debt of £2,000 takes 42 years to pay off at a standard rate of just under 20%. It will also set you back almost £5,500 in interest.

And the catch?

Ah, yes, the catch. Credit-card firms have become wise to savvy consumers like you jumping from one 0% rate to another and have started introducing balance-transfer fees.

On the back of findings that UK banks are losing roughly £1 billion a year because of card hopping, the majority of credit-card firms – but not all – now slap on a transfer fee of around 3% for moving your balance to one of its rivals. That means shifting an average debt of £4,580 between two companies could cost you almost £137.

The good news is that most of these fees are capped at £50 and so in effect the larger the amount you move the cheaper it is for you to do so. Likewise, transferring small debts may not work out to be economical. Be vigilant, however: not all card companies operate a cap. Research from the independent comparison website, www.MoneyExpert.com found that just one in eight credit-card companies now operates a ceiling on fees.

Of course, having to pay these fees is a pain, but, as we calculated earlier, your average debt of £4,580 at your average rate of 16.5% is costing you £733 a year or £550 over a nine-month period and so coughing up £50 or even £137 is not a disaster.

Other options: stable-rate cards

If dropping and swapping is not for you – and, let's face it, for many people it's not: I have friends who have enough trouble remembering to change their pants, let alone their credit cards – then you may want to consider transferring your balance to a firm that charges a low fixed rate, also known as a stable rate, for the life of your debt.

This will not be as attractive as 0% but it will be much lower than the typical APR (it's not April) and is a good compromise for those wanting to sidestep transfer fees. What needs to be remembered here, however, is that, if you use the stable-rate card to make any new purchases, those items will be charged at a steeper standard rate. The solution? Don't use stable-rate cards for anything but the transfer of your existing debts. For new purchases, get yourself another, more appropriate card – ideally one that charges you 0% interest.

Cashback and loyalty deals

According to research from the credit-card provider Morgan Stanley, people looking to trade in their credit cards pay almost as much attention to reward schemes as they do to interest rates. The firm found that, while 31% of cardholders cite interest rates as their top priority when choosing a new provider, 29% point to reward or loyalty schemes as their primary consideration.

Cashback deals, where every pound you spend is totted up at the end of the year and a proportion of that total – usually 0.5 to 1% – is returned to you by way of a cheque or credit, were named as the most popular loyalty offers, tempting 70% of those switching to reward schemes. Retail reward cards, such as Nectar cards, tempted 21% of card hoppers and were the second most popular.

The thing to remember, however, is that, if you are one of the 41% of people who carry a balance on their credit cards, you shouldn't even be thinking about reward cards. Finding the cheapest rate or taking a 0% deal should be your first priority. Some loyalty schemes are not worth the plastic they are written on. You have to spend a large amount on your cashback or loyalty card to accrue any significant rewards – in some cases just £10 for every £10,000 spent – and these gains are quickly wiped out if you are paying interest on a monthly balance at the same time.

But, if you are one of the 59% of folk who clear their credit-card balance in full every month, then these deals are perfect. Use them for as much of your usual spending as possible and build yourself up a little nest egg for the end of the year. But don't go mad. There is no point in spending more than you normally would for the sake of a 1% payout. But if you are planning any large purchases – for example, if you are buying a flat and need a new bed, sofa, or fridge – whack these items on your card.

Also worth considering are instant reward cards, which enable you to get on-the-spot discounts. The Virgin Money credit card, for example, gets you 10% off other Virgin-owned products, such as wine, train fares, flights and gym membership and, if you don't see the point in collecting points, these sorts of cards might suit you better.

As usual, there are things you need to watch out for – particularly with cashback deals. A lot of cashback rates are tiered and so, for example, you may get 1% on the first £2,000 worth of spending and then just 0.5% on anything above that. Also, some cards impose a minimum you have to spend over a certain period to qualify for any points or cashback, while some firms also stop paying cashback on purchases that take your balance over a set limit, such as £20,000.

A word of warning

Take care how you ask for information when trying to investigate the best credit-card deal. If you fail to read the small print you may find yourself authorising a series of searches of your credit report – footprints that could be left on your credit file for twelve months before they are deleted.

Future lenders may interpret an abnormal number of credit searches as evidence that you have applied for an unmanageable level of debt and might question why you have submitted an application for so much credit, ultimately kicking your application to the kerb. (Some rate hoppers also complain of providers offering them much lower credit limits.)

To avoid this, ensure that you ask only for a quotation rather than fully applying for credit when shopping around and sanction credit searches only when you are completely sure you have found yourself the right deal. Do that and you should be OK. The credit-card market is competitive and switching your card every six or twelve months should not harm your credit rating as long as you make your repayments on time and have not had more cards than you've had hot dinners.

Credit cards: things to remember
● Take full advantage of your interest-free period on purchases. Whether your bit of plastic has a 0% rate or a big fat one, you all get between 45 and 59 days' interest-free credit as long as you pay your current and

previous months' balance in full and on time. Use that time and also think about delaying major purchases until your statement date so you can take advantage of your full interest-free entitlement.

● Pay for valuable items on your card. Thanks to Section 75 of the Consumer Credit Act, if you buy something costing between £100 and £30,000 on your card, as well as items bought overseas, you can claim against your card issuer if something goes wrong with your purchases. Even if you've paid a deposit of only £10, you can claim a refund of the entire cost of the goods. So, if what you buy is damaged or faulty or doesn't turn up, or the supplier goes bust, your card issuer must make good your loss.

● Don't use your credit card to withdraw cash. Do and you'll face withdrawal charges of around 2% with a minimum charge of between £2 and £5. Withdrawing £20 could cost you a fiver, so do me a favour: use your debit card for that.

● Watch out for fines and annual fees. Pay late, even the minimum monthly amount, or exceed your credit limit (remember it's a limit, not a target) and you'll be hit with a fine. The solution: set up a direct debit to pay at least part (or all) of your bill each month. All your dropping and swapping efforts turn to dust if you rack up unnecessary costs. Also, some card firms have begun to introduce annual fees in order to offset rising bad debts and falling profits, but the vast majority of firms don't. If yours does, bye-bye.

Casebook: The card hopper

Paul Clarke, 28, from Uppingham

I have switched my credit card seven times over the last four years and I am in the process of moving once again. At the moment I owe roughly £1,500 but I have brought that down from £3,500. When I first built up that debt I wasn't earning nearly enough to pay it off, which I know was stupid, and when the introductory rate stopped and the default rate kicked in my repayments seemed astronomical.

From doing a search on Google and looking in a few newspapers I saw that there were loads of interest-free cards on the market and I thought, Why should I cripple myself each month when I can switch cards and pay nothing?

But it can be a hassle and unless you're completely organised you'll end up paying the standard rate at some point. The whole transfer process can take up to a month to sort out and if you start the process too late, as I have in the past, you'll get stung for at least one full interest payment.

And sometimes it's not always enough simply to look for the cheapest card. Many big firms manage lots of different cards and once when I tried to switch from one card to another I was told I couldn't because, unbeknown to me, the new card was owned by my old provider. I've also been turned down a couple of times but I've not really explored the reasons why.

But I would still rather go through all that than pay £30 or £40 in interest each month. Who wouldn't if they had the choice? But make sure you look around first. Don't just go for the tempting offers on the TV. Most cards give you up to a year interest-free credit now, so look at what else they can offer you, such as how low the transfer rate is or what the APR is after the 0% period ends.

Cementing the right mortgage

Without a doubt a mortgage is one of the most important loans you'll ever take out. It not only runs for many more years than any other kind of debt you might consider but is also much larger and – perhaps most importantly – it is secured. In harsh terms, that means that, if you fail to keep up with your monthly mortgage payments, your lender has the right to whip your flat or house away from you.

That makes choosing the right – and hopefully the cheapest – mortgage crucial. None of the other forms of borrowing covered in this book, such as credit cards and overdrafts, is secured. You do not need to grant Mr Provider rights to any specific assets, such as your house, car or wife/husband/partner, to take out a three-year loan or extend your overdraft. Mr Whippy cares only about your financial standing.

Secured loans have plus points, however. Not only do they mean you are able to borrow a hell of a lot more and have a much longer time to pay them off, but they will also be at cheaper rates than any other type of loan. The problem, however, is the ridiculous amount of jargon you have to wade through in order to land yourself the best mortgage deal.

For example, if I said to you, 'The rate on your three-year fixed-rate mortgage is dependent on its loan-to-value and whether or not you are subject to an early-redemption penalty with no tie-in,' you would probably want to punch me in the face and flush this book down the toilet.

And I am sure I would be a dead man if I said, 'What do you mean you went for a variable rate? Everybody knows the Bank of England is set to raise base rates three notches over the next six months. You should have fixed, my man.'

But don't be put off. It is just jargon and, once you can cut through it, getting the best mortgage deal relies on the same principles as everything else: shopping around and dropping and swapping. If the gobbledegook gets too much, however, I suggest an aspirin and a quick look at the Jargonator at the end of this section.

First things first

When it comes to mortgages your starting point is deciding how to pay back the capital. This does not involve running round the streets of London picking up litter or helping cockney grandmas across the road. Capital refers to the money borrowed, and there are two main ways to pay it off: the repayment route or the interest-only route.

The repayment route

If you don't like risk, and when it comes to your home you shouldn't, then a repayment mortgage is for you. It is the safer and more assured way to pay back the money lent to you. As safe as houses, no less.

Unlike the interest-only route, a repayment mortgage is the only way to guarantee that the property you've bought is yours at the end of the term. That means that every penny you hand over to your mortgage provider is used to pay back some of the interest due and a bit of the capital owed until the debt is finished, usually 25 years later.

At the start you pay off mostly interest and so if you sell after just one or two years you'll find you've hardly paid off any capital at all. But, over a longer period, your monthly payments eat away at larger and larger amounts of the capital borrowed. If you work in the type of job that pays out lump-sum bonuses during the year, then you should consider a flexible repayment mortgage, which allows you to pay off more than your prescribed monthly amount without incurring penalty charges. Likewise, if you are having liquidity problems (a useful term to remember when you're broke) you may want the option of taking a payment holiday.

The interest-only route

With an interest-only mortgage, all you pay the lender each month is the interest on the loan. You don't pay off any of the capital as you go along, so the size of your mortgage stays the same until the end of your mortgage term, again usually 25 years. The idea is that you make simultaneous monthly payments into some sort of investment fund, sending one lot of money off to the lender and another lot off to your chosen fund. Suitable funds include low-risk index trackers, which follow the growth (or slump) of the UK stock market and can be held within a tax-exempt individual savings account, known as an ISA; and endowment policies, which, despite being part of a huge misselling scandal, are still used by around a third of homebuyers.

The theory is that by the end of the term your investments have worked their magic and have amassed a healthy wad of cash for you to pay off the capital sum of the mortgage, with maybe even a little bit left over for you. The problem, however, is that there is no certainty in this, and, if there is a shortfall from your investments, it's your problem, not your lender's. If you make it their problem, bye-bye, home. You should only consider the interest-only route if:

- **you are a disciplined investor and are prepared to make payments into an investment scheme at the same time you pay the interest on your loan;**
- **you are considering converting to a repayment mortgage later on, which might be a suitable option if your earnings are low initially but are expected to be higher in future (for example, if you're expecting to finish some sort of training or gain a professional qualification);**
- **you are going to use a lump sum from somewhere else to pay off the capital, such as an inheritance, for example, or you plan on selling something such as another property or a business (this is usually a risky strategy, however, and waiting for someone to die is no fun);**

● **you are going to sell the mortgaged property to pay off the loan, which is possible if you don't need to live in the property, such as if it is a buy-to-let property or a second home, or if you are downsizing to something smaller or cheaper.**

If you don't fit into any of those categories then forget about interest-only mortgages. One in four of us takes out these types of mortgages, but don't jump on the bandwagon just because it is the cheaper option. Yes, borrowing £150,000 on an interest-only basis compared with a repayment basis is more than £250 a month cheaper at an interest rate of 4.84%, but don't be tempted by this just because it's the only way you can afford to get on to the housing ladder. If you are expecting to make a lot more money in the next two years or are going to divert payments into a separate fund, fine. But, if you're not, stay clear.

Casebook: Interested only in interest-only

Andrea Kapos, 32, from north London

I went for an interest-only mortgage simply because it was cheaper. It was my first step on to the housing ladder and I knew it was going to be tough financially, since I was single at the time, the flat I bought needed a bit of work and I had little or no furniture to speak of. Going for an interest-only deal gave me a bit of breathing space, since the monthly payments were roughly £250 cheaper than they would have been on a repayment basis.

I know the idea is that you're supposed to put some money by in an investment fund at the same time you pay the interest but that was never my intention. My aim was to take the cheapest route available for the first two to three years and then switch to a repayment mortgage when things had calmed down a little bit and my spending was back to normal.

The deal I went for was a variable rate that was discounted for two years but then tied me in to the lender's standard variable rate for a further twelve months after that. I am currently still within the discounted period but when that ends and I have finished my twelve payments at the standard variable rate I'm going to look around for one of the cheapest repayment rates on the market.

I could have just waited a while and saved up more money so that I was able to go for a repayment mortgage from the start, but I'm glad I didn't. In the year and nine months I've owned my flat and had my interest-only mortgage, it's gone up in price by more than £25,000. Had I waited I basically would have frozen myself out of the market and would to have looked at smaller places or cheaper areas.

Also, as I had been renting for most of the time before I bought my flat, it didn't feel strange for me to go down the interest-only route. By renting, I was flushing money down the toilet and so the interest-only route felt like a step up and allowed me to benefit from a rise in house prices.

I definitely wouldn't continue to stay on an interest-only deal in the long term unless I was saving money into some sort of investment fund – and to me that seems like a lot of hassle – but as a short-term fix I have no regrets about choosing it.

Second things second

Once you have decided on how you will repay the capital, the next step is to work out what type of interest rate you want.

Interest rates are probably the most important part of buying a house and getting it wrong could cost you thousands of pounds a year. Pay one percentage point more than the average interest rate on a flat or house worth £200,000 and it will set you back an extra £2,000 a year. Pay one percentage point less and you could *save* yourself £2,000.

The aim is to borrow the money you need for the smallest amount possible. To do that, however, you need first to work out what type of interest rate suits you best.

Standard variable rates

This is almost always the most expensive option you can go for. The standard variable rate is linked to the Bank of England's base rate (although it is usually one or two percentage points above it) and moves up and down in line with it. So, when you hear that the Bank of England has increased interest rates by a quarter of a percentage point to 5.75%, for example, then you know your variable rate is likely to go up from 6.5 or 7.5% to 6.75 or 7.75% very quickly. The thing to remember is that, when the Bank of England raises rates, lenders tend to follow suit within the blink of an eye; but, when the Bank of England *lowers* rates, providers tend to pass on that reduction in the blink of a cockney grandma crossing the road.

Fixed rates

As it says on the tin, the rate is fixed for a certain length of time and will not move if the Bank of England increases interest rates by one percentage point or 100 percentage points. This is ideal if things are tight and you need to know exactly how much you have to pay your lender each month or if you own a fully functioning crystal ball and expect interest rates to rise. If you find your crystal ball isn't working properly, however, and rates go down just as you fix your mortgage for five years, then you'll end up paying over the odds, while those on variable rates rub their hands. You also need to be careful about the type of fixed-rate deal you go for, since you may be required to move on to your lender's standard variable rate for a certain period after your fixed-rate mortgage expires. To avoid this, look for a fixed rate with no tie-ins. This will allow you to drop and swap when your two-, three- or five-year period ends.

Discounted rates

This refers to a discount on the lender's standard variable rate and is a good option for first-time buyers. Your monthly payments will still move up and down in accordance with the Bank of England's base rate but at lower levels than your provider's standard rate. A one- or two-percentage-point discount is particularly appealing if there is no tie-in period after the offer period ends. This will allow you to jump ship when the discount is over and remortgage with another lender. The bad news is that more than likely you'll be tied to your lender's variable rate for a couple of years after the discount runs out and only a large fee will allow you to escape.

Capped rates

With a capped-rate mortgage you pay the lender's standard variable rate but you are protected if interest rates climb beyond a certain level. The rate has a defined upper limit in the form of a cap and is a very good option during times of high and rising interest rates. Like fixed rates, caps make sense for those on tight budgets who need to ensure their monthly payments do not exceed a certain limit or if, like Mystic Meg, you can foresee future rate rises. If rates never reach the cap, however, you'll pay the lender's standard variable rate like everybody else.

Cashbacks

This isn't an interest-rate option but is frequently listed with other interest-rate deals and is where you get a sum of cash given back to you – often hundreds of pounds – when you take out the mortgage. This can be useful if you are buying your first place and need money upfront to buy yourself essentials such as a fridge, a bed or a high-definition wide-screen plasma TV. Cashback deals, however, will never be the cheapest and unless you need the dough don't bother.

Current-account mortgages

This basically turns your mortgage into one very large overdraft and allows you to offset all the savings you have against all the debts you owe. You essentially combine all your debts with your income so that every time your wages are paid into your account your debt pool decreases and every time you take money out your debt pool grows. The beauty of this is that while you still have to repay the loan within a set time frame – which you would do with a repayment mortgage by reducing your borrowings to zero or as you would with an interest-only mortgage by using a separate investment fund – you can over- and underpay without being penalised.

An added benefit is that the interest-rate charges for all your borrowings, such as credit-card debts, are set at the cheaper mortgage rate rather than your usual plastic rate, which could be as high as 29%. But you have to be disciplined and pay off your credit card debts as promptly as you would normally. Don't treat these debts as you would your mortgage and take 25 years to pay them off – it'll only cost you a ton in interest payments.

This route is best suited to high earners or those with a reasonably high level of savings who can also run their finances in a disciplined way. Current-account mortgages are rarely the cheapest on the market and are nearly always more expensive than the best fixed or discounted deals, but, if you want to overpay your mortgage loan at regular intervals, they make a lot of sense.

It's all in the calculation

Whatever type of interest rate you go for, make sure you ask your lender how frequently the interest is calculated. One of the biggest money spinners for a few lenders is to charge interest on your mortgage annually instead of daily. Annual calculations cost you more because, in effect, you're charged interest on money you have already paid and no longer owe. With a daily calculation your debt is recalculated at the end of each day, so that you pay interest only on the sum you still owe. Your monthly mortgage payments go directly into your account, immediately reducing your overall debt and the amount of interest chargeable.

With annual calculations, however, the amount of interest you pay is based on the outstanding loan amount at the end of the previous twelve months. That means payments made during the year will simply sit in your mortgage account rather than cut into your debt and reduce your interest. Also, if you make overpayments at any time, these will often not be credited until the end of the year.

Similarly, with a monthly calculated interest mortgage, a payment made on the first day of the month will not reduce the amount you owe until the last day of that month. In numbers, that means that, if you took out a £200,000 mortgage at a standard variable rate of 7%, calculated on a daily basis, you would repay almost £422,000 over 25 years, whereas the same mortgage calculated annually would set you back some £429,000 – an extra £7,000.

Third things third

Once you have decided how you intend to pay back the capital and which particular interest rate suits your needs the most, the all-important next step is to find yourself the cheapest deal.

Again, the best way to do this is to get online, flick through the money sections of the national newspapers or buy yourself a specialist financial magazine to find out which mortgage deals are at the top of the best-buy tables. But this is not as easy as it sounds and so I have prepared a mock table to help you on your way.

If, for example, you've decided you want a repayment mortgage at a fixed rate because you believe interest rates are likely to go up or because things are tight and you need to know exactly how much you have to pay your lender each month, you need to browse the fixed-rate tables, which will look a little something like this:

Fixed rates with no extended redemption tie-in

Lender	Rate %	Period	Max LTV	Fee	Incentive
Fat Belly bank	5.25	for 2 yrs	80%	£999	No HLC
Chubby bank	5.49	for 2 yrs	95%	£449	No HLC, 6 mths' free ASU
Big-Boned bank	5.75	for 5 yrs	95%	£499	No HLC

As you can see, Fat Belly bank is top of the table offering a fixed rate of 5.25% for two years with no tie-in after the two years are up. In simple terms that means you can jump ship after the fixed-rate period ends and are not obliged to transfer to Fat Belly bank's standard variable rate for any length of time. The snag with this deal is that you have to pay an arrangement fee of £999, the largest of any of the three deals.

A further problem with Fat Belly bank's deal is that you need a whopping 20% deposit. *Max LTV* (loan to value) refers to the maximum amount a provider will lend you in relation to the value of the home you want. If your home is priced at £100,000 Fat Belly bank will lend you 80% of that or £80,000, which means you have to come up with the other £20,000. Big-Boned bank's deal meanwhile has an LTV of 95% and so you need to stump up a deposit of only £5,000 on the same £100,000 property.

Using all this information, you then need to decide which deal is right for you. If you have only a small deposit, Fat Belly bank's offer is no good, and if you are worried about fixing your rate for a very long period of time – possibly because you believe interest rates might fall after two years – then Big-Boned bank's offer is not the one for you.

Thankfully, none of the three deals carries a higher lending charge, which is what *No HLC* means. Higher lending charges, also known as a mortgage indemnity premium or MIP, are one-off fees lenders sometimes charge if you want to borrow a high percentage of your property's value. Try to avoid these charges at all times.

If none of these things matters to you and it is just a question of which deal is the cheapest, you need to make sure you add up all the costs. For example, borrowing £100,000 from Fat Belly bank will cost you £606 a month and £14,544 over a two-year fixed term. If you add the £999 arrangement fee to this, the total cost of Fat Belly bank's deal is £15,543. Chubby bank's deal, meanwhile, adds up to £15,329, including the arrangement fee, while Big-Boned bank's costs £15,576 over two years, although you have to remember that you are locked into this deal for five years.

So, despite Fat Belly bank's deal being top of the pops, it is not in fact the cheapest, Chubby bank's is, and you also get six months' free accident, sickness and unemployment cover, shown as *6mths' free ASU*. So, whatever interest rate you go for, whether it's a variable, capped or discounted rate, it is crucial you add up all the costs of a particular offer before deciding which one is right for you.

A word of warning: when rates don't add up

Best-buy tables are great when it comes to dropping and swapping, but beware of rock-bottom mortgage rates. Providers can and will manipulate their rates to get to the top of best-buy tables, because they know savvy consumers like you use them to search for the cheapest offers.

The mortgage market is very competitive and being top of the best buys can be very lucrative for a lender. Consequently, more and more are chopping their headline rates in order to make their deals appear more attractive than they actually are, while slyly recouping revenue by slapping on hefty fees.

According to research from Moneyfacts, the independent financial-research firm, there are almost 250 mortgages on the market that charge an arrangement, booking or completion fee in excess of £499, of which more than 60 – either via flat or percentage fees – slap on charges in excess of £999. So be careful. Don't look only at headline rates when scouring the market; and take into account any additional fees and tot up all the costs before making your decision.

A word on re-mortgaging

If you are not a first-time buyer and already have an existing mortgage, you need to bear in mind that dropping and swapping may not only require you to pay an arrangement fee to your new provider but may also require you to cough up an exit fee to your existing Fat Belly bank.

If you are tied into a special-rate deal with Mr Lender, you will need to cross his palm with more than a few gold coins to be able to move to one of his rivals, and this will be on top of any fixed closure fees. The remedy? Make sure you consider all these costs before masterminding your switch.

But, if you have a loan of £200,000 and your current mortgage rate is two percentage points higher than the cheapest market rates, it is costing you an extra £4,000 a year to stay where you are. The fees incurred by dropping and swapping will most probably be in the region of £1,000 so – depending on your current rate – it is still a very sensible move.

And, if you are moving a repayment mortgage with fifteen years to run, make sure you switch into an equivalent fifteen-year deal and not a 25-year offer. A 25-year deal will be much cheaper on a monthly basis but you'll end up being hit for ten more years of payments. And that punch will hurt.

It may also be worth talking to your existing provider first before you exit, since it's amazing how generous it can be when Fat Belly bank thinks you might be heading for one of its competitors. If you are lucky they'll put you on one of the cheaper deals they offer new customers, saving yourself a lot of time, hassle and fees.

Eight mortgage options to help you get a leg up

With the average price of a house now almost £180,000 and our average yearly incomes more than seven times lower at £25,000, it is getting harder than ever before to get on to the housing ladder. Banks, buildings societies and other providers will typically lend you three to four times your gross salary and up to three times a joint income if you are buying with your partner. But that still leaves many of us woefully short of what we need. To get around that, here are eight mortgage options that might help you bridge the gap.

1. Longer mortgage periods

You can reduce your monthly payments and therefore afford to borrow more by extending the life of your loan. Research from www.MoneyExpert.com found that nearly a third of UK lenders now allow borrowers to take out a mortgage lasting 40 years or more, with a couple of firms offering deals stretching out more than 50 years. In numbers that means that someone borrowing £180,000 at 5% over 40 years on a repayment basis would pay back £867 a month compared with £1,052 a month over 25 years.

The downside: It costs you. Someone taking out the £180,000 loan on the same terms for 40 years would pay back a whopping £416,616 including interest compared with £315,678 over 25 years.

2. Buy-to-share

Renting a spare room to a friend or colleague has long been a popular way to help first-time buyers keep up with their monthly mortgage payments, but a few lenders now allow borrowers to add £6,375 – the amount you can earn from renting out two rooms in your house or flat before you have to pay income tax – to their annual income. Based on a standard four-times-income mortgage, that means you would be able to borrow an additional £25,500 to put towards your dream house.

The downside: Sharing with a stranger and potentially having to clean toenail clippings out of the sink.

3. Buying with mates

More and more people are buying with friends or family members in a bid to get a foot up. Websites are even popping up to bring together strangers who want to buy. It is a nice solution for singletons to be able to club their salaries together and enjoy the same spending power as couples.

The downside: This can put a strain on your friendship and if you fall out there is a lot more at stake than just losing a drinking partner. Those buying together should consider doing so on a tenants-in-common basis. This allows you to split the property into whatever size of shares you want, avoiding disputes when you come to selling.

4. Rent-to-buy

This route allows tenants to save for a property while they are renting. The tenant agrees to pay a premium on top of their rent, usually 10%, which is put towards a deposit for the property. You also need to pay an option fee up front, which confirms your right to buy for an agreed sum at the end of a fixed period, typically three to five years. The beauty of this route is that you are insured against rising house prices and can buy the property for the price the home was valued at when you first started renting.

The downside: You'll need to be able to afford your monthly rental payments as well as the 10% on top. Fail to pay that more than once and your right to buy disappears. You also need to make sure you can afford the mortgage payments once you do buy.

5. Five-times-income mortgages

A couple of mortgage providers hit the headlines after announcing they were to offer loans based on five times people's salaries. This is good news for those of us struggling to keep up with spiking house prices, although only a few of us actually qualify for such loans, as providers want you to have deposits of at least 25%, a household income that is around double the national average, a spotlessly clean credit record and low outgoings.

The downside: You run the risk of taking on more debt than you can actually afford while few first-time buyers will qualify.

6. Shared ownership schemes

HomeBuy, the government scheme developed in conjunction with private-sector lenders, has been set up to help key workers, social tenants and priority first-time buyers to secure their first home. Under the initiative, homebuyers take out a mortgage for 75% of the property's value from one of four lenders as well as an interest-free loan on the remaining 25% from that lender and the government. The loan is paid back when the property is resold with the amount paid back being 25% of the value of the property at the time of sale.

The downside: The Royal Institute of Chartered Surveyors says the scheme has little impact on first-time house sales and will account for fewer than 1% of transactions per year, benefiting only 20,000 buyers over five years. Mortgage rates are also higher than the cheapest mortgages available to other first-time buyers.

7. 100% mortgages

Research from Abbey, the high-street bank, shows that close to 7 million first-time buyers are unable to get on the housing ladder because they can't afford the deposit. As a result, more and more lenders are offering 100% mortgages. Some lenders are also offering 125% mortgages with the idea being that you put the extra money towards furniture or other costs such as legal fees and stamp duty. Unlike 100% offers, however, 125% deals require you to put down a deposit of at least 5% of the value of your property.

The downside: 100% mortgages are expensive. Basically the larger the deposit you can put down the cheaper your mortgage becomes and this route is the antithesis of that. Also, if property prices fall you will be instantly submerged into negative equity, whereby your home is worth less than the amount you borrowed to pay for it.

8. Guarantor mortgages

Parents or a rich uncle or aunt can guarantee your mortgage for you, allowing you to borrow more. Some lenders will ask that your rich uncle guarantees the full amount of the loan, while others ask for the difference between the amount you can pay and the purchase price to be guaranteed.

The downside: Again, these deals are not as cheap as the best fixed or variable rates on the market, and not everyone has a family member with deep pockets and long fingers.

What's all the fuss with endowments?

In theory, an endowment policy, which is a combination of life assurance, savings and investments, is supposed to grow above and beyond what you need to repay your mortgage – leaving you with a bonus to spend on whatever you like.

Like Wham!, they were extremely popular in the 1980s, when interest rates were historically high, inflation was roaring and you received tax relief on the premiums you paid into your policy. Sadly, these endowments have failed to meet the expectations of thousands of borrowers because the charges on these policies were too high and deteriorating market conditions put pressure on investment returns.

The upshot is that many people's endowments are not producing anywhere near enough to pay back the capital borrowed on their mortgages, let alone any extra for something nice.

This problem has been compounded by the fact that people were told their policies would, 100%, be enough to pay off their mortgages. A Treasury Select Committee report suggests that as many as 60% of all endowment policies bought may have been sold with false promises.

This has become known as the endowment misselling scandal and thankfully those who were not informed of the risks associated with using an endowment at the time they bought their policies have grounds for complaint and should be able to claim compensation from their insurer. If that includes you, time is running out, however. You have either six years from when you bought your policy or three years from the date you realised it may have been missold to you to make a complaint. You should first approach the company who sold you the endowment and if that doesn't work out your next step should be to contact the Financial Ombudsman Service (South Quay Plaza, 183 Marsh Wall, London E14 9SR; 0845 080 1800).

Which? also provides excellent advice at www.endowmentaction.co.uk, which includes details of whom to complain to and how to do it – including letters you can print off to make an instant complaint.

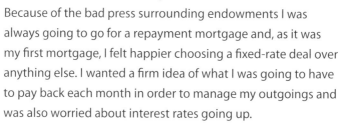

Casebook: The fixer

Lydia Christie, 31, from Brighton

Because of the bad press surrounding endowments I was always going to go for a repayment mortgage and, as it was my first mortgage, I felt happier choosing a fixed-rate deal over anything else. I wanted a firm idea of what I was going to have to pay back each month in order to manage my outgoings and was also worried about interest rates going up.

I eventually decided on a two-year fixed deal rather than a three-year fixed rate because the interest on the three-year offer was slightly higher and the arrangement fee was slightly bigger. In hindsight, however, I wish I had gone for the three-year option because interest rates have actually gone up three times since I took out my mortgage and I'm worried about the extra I'll have to pay when my deal runs out.

To find the best rate I initially went to see a mortgage adviser recommended by an estate agent, but the rates offered to me were far worse than those I had seen at the top of the best-buy tables in the weekend newspapers, and I suspected I was being shown only a limited number of deals.

I trusted the best-buy tables more. They listed the main terms of each deal, such as the interest rate, how long the fixed rate lasted and what fees were payable, as well as the contact details of the mortgage provider, and so I simply called up a provider at the top of one of the tables, answered a few questions and was sent an application form through the post. A couple of weeks later I had a mortgage, fixed for two years with no tie-in after that.

But I was lucky that the provider I went for was flexible. Having never bought a property or applied for a mortgage before, I was not entirely sure how long the whole process of buying a property would take and my mortgage offer was valid for only three months. Unfortunately, my flat purchase stalled because of some toing and froing with the seller and the mortgage offer period expired. The problem was that interest rates had gone up in the meantime and I was worried I would be offered a higher fixed rate or be told to pay a fee to keep my old rate. Luckily, neither happened, but I know other providers might not have done the same.

Fixing really turned out to be the right move for me, considering that rates have already gone up. My only complaint, as I've said, is that I wish I'd fixed for longer.

The Jargonator

Base rate: The interest rate set by the Bank of England, used as a basis for the rates that the Fat Belly banks offer their customers. The base rate can go down as well as up.

Buy-to-let mortgage: A special mortgage for a property that will be let to tenants.

Capital: The amount you have borrowed on your mortgage and on which interest is charged.

Current-account mortgage: A flexible mortgage with a daily interest calculation that has a bank account attached to it. Money in the bank account is offset against the outstanding balance of the mortgage on a daily basis.

Early-redemption penalty: The financial penalty you have to pay for fully repaying your mortgage or making a lump-sum reduction of the balance.

Endowment: A form of life insurance that pays a tax-free lump sum at the end of its term or a guaranteed amount – usually the mortgage debt – in the event of the policyholder's death.

Equity: The total value of your property less the amount of the mortgage. If your house is worth £200,000 and you have a mortgage of £150,000, your equity is £50,000.

Interest: The money you are charged for borrowing.

Interest calculation: The frequency with which lenders calculate the outstanding balance on mortgages annually, monthly or daily.

Loan to value (LTV): A percentage figure indicating the size of the mortgage on a property in relation to its value. For example, a house worth £200,000 with a mortgage of £100,000 would have an LTV of 50%. Better mortgage deals are available for lower LTVs – 75% and below.

Mortgage-indemnity premium: Sometimes called a higher lending charge, this is a one-off fee that borrowers may be charged if they want to borrow a high percentage of a property's value – usually above 90% or 95% of the asking price.

Mortgage term: The length of time over which the mortgage will be repaid.

Negative equity: When your home is worth less than the amount you borrowed to pay for it.

Redemption: The paying off of a mortgage loan.

Security: The property the mortgage is being used to buy is the lender's security for the loan. This means that the lender has rights over the property. If the mortgage repayments are not kept up to date, the lender can repossess the property and sell it to recover the debt.

Stamp duty: A government tax on buying properties costing more than £60,000.

Split loan: A mortgage that has some of the loan set up on an interest-only basis and some on a repayment basis.

Standard variable rate (SVR): Lenders' SVRs fluctuate at their discretion as economic conditions change.

Title deeds: The legal documents that set out the ownership of a property.

Tracker mortgage: These are schemes with a variable rate set above or below the Bank of England's base rate.

Getting personal with your loans

Want to buy something now but don't have the money immediately at hand to pay for it? Want the security of knowing exactly how much you will have to pay back each month? Planning to buy something such as a car but are reluctant to pay on hire purchase, where what you've bought will belong to the credit company until you've made your final payment? Want me to stop asking questions?

Fine. All I'm trying to get at is that, if any of these questions describe your situation, then an unsecured personal loan might be the most suitable form of borrowing for you – as long as you shop around, dammit.

For many small and medium-sized purchases, running from a couple of hundred to a few thousand pounds, unsecured loans can be the most appropriate form of credit. The rates are fixed, so you can budget around your monthly payments; the debt is not tied to any item – such as a property – meaning that only your credit rating and not your home is at risk; and – unlike the case with a mortgage – you can set the life of your loan over a shorter period so you're not saddled with a hefty long-term debt.

But, before you speed off down the information superhighway to find the market's cheapest deals, think carefully about whether or not you need a personal loan at all. Looking at the current best-buy tables for unsecured personal loans, you'll see that the cheapest rates you'll get for borrowing £7,500 over five years is between 7 and 8% – and that is dependent on you having a credit rating so clean you can see your face in it. A better solution might be to open a 0% credit card instead.

If you need the money to pay for a holiday and know you'll have enough cash to pay the loan back after six to ten months, then opening a credit card that offers a 0% interest rate on new purchases is a much better and cheaper option than taking out a personal loan at 8%.

Even if you want to use the loan to pay off an expensive overdraft or cure a cash-flow problem you can still do this with a credit card. All you do is ring up your new credit-card provider and ask them to transfer the credit limit from your card to your bank account. Some credit-card companies will allow you to transfer your entire credit limit while others will allow you to transfer a proportion, such as 90 or 95% of your credit ceiling.

But you have to be disciplined. If the 0% rate on your new credit card runs out in ten months, you have to make sure you've paid back the amount you've borrowed within that timeframe or made arrangements to drop and swap to another 0% card before. There is no point exposing yourself to your lender's non-introductory rate, which could be as high as 20% – you'll just turn all your good work to jelly. (If your lender's non-introductory rate is 20%, however, exposing yourself – after a week without washing – might be satisfying.)

If that all sounds like too much hassle, however, or you need to borrow more than a credit-card limit allows, then a personal loan might suit you better. But, as with any other form of debt, there are things you need to watch out for.

What should I look out for?

Typical rates: So you've shopped around, got online, flicked through a couple of the money sections of the national newspapers and have found a personal-loan rate that makes you go weak at the knees. The bad news is the rate you've been wooed by might not be the one you end up being offered.

As many as 80% of personal-loan providers use risk-based pricing to work out the rate they'll offer you and crucial to this is your credit history. A firm might advertise a typical rate of 7% but if your credit score is slightly soiled the rate you actually get could be more than double that.

The rules of the game say that providers are allowed to advertise a 7% typical rate as long as two-thirds of accepted customers are offered that rate. That might, however, leave you among the 33% of people who get smacked in the face with a higher rate.

The real kicker is that you find out the rate you're offered only *after* you've formally applied for the loan, creating an additional search on your credit file. To get round this, make sure you check the small print. The best-buy tables should inform you whether or not an advertised rate is dependent on your credit record, and if it is, and you know your credit score is patchy, stay clear. Better to search around for a cheaper guaranteed rate.

Redemption penalties: If you think there is any chance that you might want to repay your loan early – either because you're expecting a bonus or an inheritance, or you want to move to another lender – then make sure you go for one of the few loans with no redemption penalty, or at best make sure you haven't signed up to a loan with particularly high redemption charges. Knowledge is power, so make sure you read the small print and ask questions before you apply.

Payment-protection insurance: Like *Grange Hill*'s Zammo, you should just say no to payment-protection insurance (PPI) – it is expensive, often unnecessary and statistically you are unlikely to make a successful claim. PPI covers repayments if you have an accident, get sick or are made redundant, but according to research fewer than one in 20 policies results in a claim and, of those that do, as many as 85% are kicked to the kerb. Aggressive salesmen heavily push PPI because it is a big money spinner for them, and, unless you specify that you don't want it, you'll end up getting it. PPI is not compulsory, so make sure you ask Chubby bank if it has been included within the cost of your loan quote. If you do need this type of insurance, and it's fair to say that some of you will, then shop around – particularly online where you can sidestep the sales pitch – for an alternative accident, sickness and unemployment policy.

Repayment period: Borrow for a longer period and you will pay back more in interest. It's that simple. In some cases it might suit you to borrow over ten years rather than five, because extending your loan period makes your monthly payments smaller and more manageable. But, if you *can* pay back the money over a shorter timeframe, make sure you do. Do you really want to be paying off your holiday to Spain five years after you get back? You'll have no tan to speak of and will have long forgotten about Enrique's or Lucita's tight buns, leaving the lump sum Fat Belly bank is whipping out of your account each month as your only holiday memory.

Loan size: Be aware of loan tiers. With any other kind of debt, such as a mortgage or racking up expenses on your credit card, the more you borrow, the more you'll pay back. But, with personal loans, applying for a few more pounds could actually save you money. This is because many loan providers operate a tiered pricing structure, offering lower rates for larger advances and much higher rates for small loans. For example, borrow £3,000 from some providers and you'll be charged rates of around 20%. Borrow more than £10,000 from the same providers, however, and they'll offer you rates up to two-thirds cheaper. But don't go mad. There's no need to borrow an extra £7,000 just to take advantage of a cheaper rate. Just be aware of how your Podgy provider tiers it rates. Borrowing £4,999 might be calculated at a rate of 15% while borrowing just £1 more could reduce it to 8%.

Consolidated loans: I've seen them on the TV but what are they?

Debt consolidation is the process by which a single loan is taken out to pay off all your other existing loans. This can be done to obtain a lower interest rate, making your monthly repayments smaller, or to simplify your repayment plans. Unlike debt management, where your previous debts are not cleared, a consolidation loan pays off all your old debts to leave you with one shiny, hulking new one.

This can be done by converting all your existing unsecured loans into one unsecured loan; or, more typically (and a lot more dangerously), grouping your debts into a secured loan, which is guaranteed against an asset – usually your home. Because secured loans offer less risk to the Podgy providers, it sometimes means the interest rates on consolidated loans are lower than on some unsecured debts. If you fail to pay it off, however, your house or flat will disappear faster than you can say, 'Have you ever thought about consolidating your loans into one easy-to-manage monthly payment?'

Should I do it?

In a word: no. Secured loans should be lending of the last resort. The consolidation ads you'll have seen on daytime TV, which compete with the ones about tripping over in the workplace, make secured debt look as if it were something for everyone. It's not. For a very select number of people, who have already explored all their other borrowing options, it can be. For the overwhelming majority of us, however, they should be avoided.

OK, but why?

The lender gets the security – not you. The majority of consolidated loans are secured and that's bad. The word *secured* wrongly gives us the impression that these loans are safer or we are more protected in some way. Wrong! Turn your credit-card debts into secured debts and you put your home on the line, not just your credit rating. They should be renamed *vulnerable loans*.

Rates are variable not fixed

Unlike that of an unsecured loan, the rate you have to pay is not fixed for the life of the debt. Unsecured loans give you the security of knowing exactly how much you have to pay back each month. Your outgoings don't change, allowing you to budget around your monthly payments. But the rates on secured loans are variable and your Podgy provider can change them as and when it chooses – leaving you with far less certainty.

Lending is extended over a longer period

With secured loans you're encouraged to borrow over much longer periods, sometimes 25 years. This is massively longer than the normal unsecured loan that you're replacing. This is how your Podgy provider gets away with advertising 'one low easy payment'. It's lower, not because interest rates are lower – they won't be, but because you're going to be paying it off for what'll seem like forever. Let's make this absolutely clear. An unsecured loan of £10,000 at a 15% interest rate paid back over five years will set you back around £4,000 in interest. A secured loan at a lower rate of 12.9% over 25 years will strip you of £22,000.

Larger borrowing

Because your debts are secured, loan companies will allow you to borrow much more than the debts you are consolidating. This is very dangerous. What you need is *cheaper* debt, not *more* debt, and consolidated loans rarely provide that.

So whom does it suit?

For those with very high levels of credit-card and particularly store-card debt, which charge average interest rates of around

30%, a consolidated loan may be the answer – but only if you have explored all your other options. If you are faced with a situation where consolidating your loans could save you from being declared bankrupt, fine. But if you have other alternatives, explore them first.

What are my other options?

Look at credit-card balance transfers: If you have debts on credit cards, and a decent credit score, then using a credit card to consolidate your debts is by far the cheapest way to act. It is possible to shift debts to a card that offers you a permanent, long-term rate of around 4%, or open a card with a 0% interest rate for a fixed period. Be aware that you need to pay your debts off before that 0% period ends, however. Or at least make plans to drop and swap to another 0% offer.

Consider remortgaging or adding debts on to your mortgage: A mortgage is effectively a secured loan for your house, except that, at rates of usually 5.5% to 7.5%, it's massively cheaper. It's often possible simply to shift debts on to your mortgage at this cheap rate or, if you have equity in your home, you could consider remortgaging to release capital to pay back your debts. This will also extend your indebtedness over a longer period but at a much cheaper interest rate.

Check out a normal unsecured personal loan: These are by and large cheaper than secured loans and your home isn't at risk – the cheapest are at around 7%. Check out the best-buy tables in the weekend newspapers or get online to find them.

Use any savings you have to repay your debt: The interest paid on savings is usually far less than the interest charged on borrowing. If you have any savings it is generally much better to use these to pay off your debts first.

Think twice about taking out a loan if …

- It's the last untapped source of borrowing. If your credit cards are maxed out and your overdraft is so far into the red that your statements arrive in purple envelopes you might be wise to forget about it.

- You just want it for a spur-of-the-moment purchase. Couldn't that top-of-the-range car stereo with its removable flip-front panel, iPod plug-in and ten-CD changer wait until someone has nicked your current one?

- You need to put it down as a deposit on a property you are buying. If property prices fall you will be instantly plunged into negative equity with your home being worth less than the amount you borrowed to pay for it.

- You've seen an ad on TV offering you a seemingly unbeatable loan rate. Chances are it won't be. Avoid the temptation and make sure you shop around first. Also, think about watching more BBC 1 and BBC 2.

- Your lenders are giving you an increasingly hard time about paying your debts back. The simple solution is not to borrow more but to reduce your spending. Get into walking, making sandwiches for lunch and swapping Georgio Armani for George at Asda.

Overdrafts: swimming into the light

Here are some numbers. 30 million of us have overdraft facilities linked to our bank accounts, 14 million of us make regular use of them, 3.5 million of us are permanently overdrawn, 2 million of us exceed our overdraft limits at least 4 times a year, and – perhaps most worryingly – another 2 million of us are still overdrawn the minute we get paid.

To cut a lot of numbers short, we jointly owe some £10 billion in overdraft debt, an amount that has more than doubled over the last six years, and are paying charges that rather annoyingly generate £3 billion a year for the Fat Belly banks.

The trouble is that overdrafts have become an everyday part of life and are no longer treated as the short-term borrowing facility they were once designed to be. They have gone from being a tool used in an emergency to something 3.5 million of us use on a permanent basis. The real kicker, however, is that it is costing the 2 million of us who regularly exceed our overdraft limits almost £300 a year in penalty charges.

The problem? We have become complacent. According to a report commissioned by the online bank Egg, more than 60% of us have no idea how much money is in our accounts at any one time, causing many of us unknowingly to exceed our agreed overdraft limits, while a study from price-comparison company uSwitch found that we wrongly believe the annual interest rate on our authorised overdrafts is just 4.5% when in fact for the big five high-street banks – HSBC, (RBS) NatWest, Lloyds TSB, HBOS and Barclays – it's actually closer to 17%.

For some reason – maybe because our overdrafts are linked to our current accounts – we are not as vigilant with this type of borrowing as we are with our other debts and are much more likely to put up with outrageously high fees, ridiculous rates of interest and stinking customer service. Like Madonna, we have got into the groove of shopping around and dropping and swapping when it comes to our credit-card and mortgage debts but seem to love being treated badly when it comes to overdrafts.

But it doesn't make sense. A Chubby bank will happily hit you for £30 a time for going over your agreed overdraft limit and will then cheerfully make you pay its unauthorised lending rate of up to 30%. Some Fat Belly banks will even charge you their higher unauthorised borrowing rate on your total outstandings if you exceed your overdraft limit by just a penny. Unbelievable. That means if you push your agreed overdraft of £1,000 up to £1,000.01 you may be hit with rates of 30% on everything you owe, not just the penny that broke Fat Belly's back.

Once you are beyond your agreed overdraft limit, meanwhile, your bank suddenly remembers it is under no obligation to cover any further transactions and will gleefully bounce cheques, reject standing orders and decline direct debits on your behalf. At a cost, of course. Thirty-two pounds a time, on average, according to the advice website www.MoneyExpert.com.

So what to do?

The good news is that these problems are easily rectifiable. If you slip into the red on a regular basis, choose a current account that offers a low overdraft rate. Simple. Overdrafts are a massive money spinner for British banks but a little forward planning, such as arranging a bigger overdraft facility when you know your spending is going to be higher than usual – around Christmas and New Year, for example – should help you avoid punitive overdraft charges. Also, call your bank as soon as you've fallen into the red and ask for a temporary overdraft or a borrowing increase. With any luck, this will prevent a flurry of charges hitting your account.

Many high-street and online banks, as well as building societies, also offer interest-free buffer overdrafts of up to £500, so, if you regularly slip into the red, look at switching over to one of these.

The problem is that 65% of us stay with our existing current-account providers because we think transferring our direct debits and standing orders is too much hassle, according to a survey by the high-street bank, Abbey. The bank also found another 16% of us believe we are unable to switch because we are overdrawn. Rubbish.

It is vital you kick the habit of staying loyal to your existing provider. The much-overused statistic that we are more likely to change our partner than we are our bank is embarrassing. But the fact is the rates and fees attached to some overdrafts are shocking and it is high time you got a divorce.

And it's not difficult to do. If you want to jump ship you can hand over the hassle of transferring your direct debits and standing orders to the switching team at your new bank, which will automatically arrange these transfers for you within ten working days. And don't believe you are unattractive to another bank or building society just because you are overdrawn. Banks are making £3 billion a year from the charges we pay on our overdrafts, plus a further £1.1 billion in interest charges, so remember: you are just as valuable to lenders as someone who is constantly in the black, if not more so.

But where do I find the best deals?

As with any other form of debt you need to get online, flick through the national newspapers or read a few specialist financial magazines to find out which overdraft deals are the best.

In the money sections of Sunday newspapers or websites such as www.fool.co.uk, www.uswitch.com and www.thisismoney.com

you'll find a host of best-buy tables that will point you to Internet banks which, up to certain limits, will take on your existing overdraft at rates of 0% for an initial twelve-month period before putting you on a long-term rate of around 7%; or to branch-based lenders that'll offer 0% rates for the first year before applying long-term rates of around 9%.

But be aware of what you are signing up to. To get the best rates you may have to fund your account with anything between £500 to £1,000 a month, while some accounts will offer you only a 0% rate on the first £2,500 or £5,000 of your overdraft before charging the remainder at its standard rate. Always read the small print.

Eight ways to avert overdraft fees

1. **Make sure you always know the true balance of your account. It is easy to forget what you've spent, particularly after a boozy Friday or Saturday night, so make a note.**

2. **Talk to your bank. If you know there is a chance a payment will be made late, get it off your chest. Let Fat Belly bank know you are about to go overdrawn and it might waive any late fees. It doesn't always work but providers are generally more lenient if you keep them in the loop.**

3. **No matter how tempting, do not write cheques before you have the money in your account. Some shops scan your cheque and drain the cash from your account on the day it is written.**

4. **Keep up to date with your debit-card transactions. Money is often debited from your account three days after your purchase is made, so be aware of that. Also, just because a transaction is approved, it doesn't mean you have the cash in your account to cover it.**

5. **Easier said than done, but try to keep a few extra hundred pounds in your account as a buffer. If you choose the right current account with a competitive interest rate, you'll also get a decent return on your buffer fund.**

6. **Get online.** There is little worse than queuing at your local Chubby bank to pay a bill – you are too busy for that. Your online bank never sleeps, it doesn't close at weekends and you won't be asked to take a seat – making you less likely to miss a payment.

7. **Organise your direct debits and standing orders to come out of your bank on the day you get paid.** Delay payments until too long after pay day and there is a high chance you'll have no money left in your account to cover them.

8. **Make sure your bank has your updated personal information,** including address, phone number and email address, so it can contact you straight away if you slip into the red.

Taking back what's yours

If you have racked up a large amount of penalty charges from your provider and just moving to one of its rivals is not sweet enough justice for you, then you could try getting those charges back. It sounds like a long shot but 85% of people have been successful, according to *Which?*.

Under the Unfair Terms in Consumer Contracts Regulations, penalty charges – including the £40 your bank hit you with for having to inform you it bounced one of your cheques – genuinely have to reflect the cost of administering them.

The law says these fees must not be a profit-making activity and have instead to be proportional to the actual costs of administration. In simple terms, if the letter you received to inform you that you had exceeded your overdraft limit was written with golden ink and was hand-delivered by Michael Jackson then a £40 charge would seem fair. For an automated letter through the post, however, there is an argument it's illegal.

And it is this point – that banking charges are far higher than their cost of administration – that has enabled thousands of savvy consumers to successfully recover hundreds and sometimes thousands of pounds from the bellies of their fat banks.

Experts estimate that the highest cost that banks could justify for bouncing cheques is £4.50, while for other items, such as declining direct debits or standing orders, the highest cost is judged to be in the region of £2.50. No bank has been willing to declare the actual costs of these transactions but that hasn't stopped many of the well-known high-street names from returning a heap of money to thousands of angry customers.

If you think you have been a victim of what some are calling bank robbery, then here is a quick guide to help you reclaim your bank charges. You should also refer to www.penaltycharges.co.uk, www.bbc.co.uk/themoneyprogramme and www.moneysavingexpert.com for excellent advice and assistance on how to recover unfair costs.

The plan

First of all you need to find out and total up all your charges. According to UK law the maximum period of time you can backdate and reclaim money is six years, so you need to find out all the fees you've been hit for during that time.

If you've got all your bank statements, highlight all of your charges, make copies and send them as well as a covering letter (use gold ink if you can) to your bank asking for the money to be returned. If you need help constructing the cover letter, templates can be found and downloaded at all three of the above websites.

If you don't have all your bank statements, then you can submit an estimated claim if you genuinely believe you have been charged during a period for which you have no details. If one year's statements show £100 of charges, you can estimate the total amount of charges for six years to be £600.

If you don't have any statements at all, you can also send a letter to your bank requesting a complete list of all previous charges – it's your legal right to do this under the Data Protection Act, although your bank is allowed to charge you for this so be prepared to part with a fee of around £10.

The next step is to post your letter, including a photocopy of your highlighted statement, by recorded delivery to your lender's branch address. Your bank will probably respond to the letter by either refusing to meet your claim or by offering to settle in part or, if you're very lucky, in full.

If the claim is small, your lender may want to settle it quickly to reduce its legal and administrative costs. If the claim is large, it is more likely it will do nothing – waiting until you actually go ahead and file a claim at court.

If, after fourteen days, you've received no response, or are unhappy with your bank's response, your next step is to file a claim. There's a fee of between £30 and £120, depending on the size of your claim, to do so but if your bank coughs up this fee will be refunded. You can access a claim form at all of the three web addresses above. When you file a claim, you are also entitled to apply for interest on all the penalty charges your bank has levied against you – from the date they were originally deducted from your account.

Your Fat Belly bank is then obliged to defend its case before the judge or else pay the amount you are claiming. If it chooses not to defend itself, a very common outcome, you automatically win by default after fourteen days and, as well as paying the full amount of your claim, your bank will also refund your court fee.

So far (at the time of writing) no lender has defended their penalty charges in court – possibly because they don't want to set a precedent if they lose or because they're afraid of revealing their true costs – but that doesn't mean one won't in future. A standard has not been set on this and the banks are furiously developing their policies to fight back.

There's no guarantee you'll win but – so far – the majority of people who have tried have been successful. It's well worth the effort if you believe you've been hit by one too many unfair charges.

Overdrafts: in numbers

Although the average overdraft balance in the UK is £677, it's 68% higher for men at around £867, compared with £515 for women. And it's not just those of us on lower incomes making use of overdrafts. According to uSwitch almost a third of people with an annual income in excess of £40,000 use an overdraft with one in nine permanently overdrawn. At the same time, uSwitch found that 1.8 million 18 to 29-year-olds are permanently overdrawn with more than a fifth admitting to owing in excess of £1,000. The average overdraft among this age group is £656.

PART 2:
SAVE IT

Rainy days, here I come

Two conflicting schools of thought exist when it comes to saving: one is that you should first pay off all your debts before you even think about putting money away for a rainy day; the other is that you should save at least something from your monthly salary, however little, to get you into the habit of setting money aside.

The first point would seem fair enough. It makes no sense putting £1,000 into a savings account – even one of the better ones, which pays interest of around 5.5% – if you owe £10,000 on a store card that charges you 30% a year interest. Your savings will magic you little more than £174 over three years while putting the £1,000 towards your £10,000 credit-card debt will have saved you £2,197.

That is an extreme example, however. Yes, Britain's personal debt is increasing by £1 million every four minutes but that doesn't mean you have to wait until you are completely debt-free before you start saving your cash.

If your debts consist of just a mortgage or carry very low interest charges, such as a student loan, there is no need to delay your savings drive. The majority of you will be paying off your mortgage for many more years to come and will be able to beat the rates you are being charged on your student debts with your savings rates. Likewise, if you've taken to heart the concept of dropping and swapping and have been savvy enough to move your credit-card or overdraft debts to a 0% rate provider – there are plenty out there – you should also be tucking money away.

OK, but how much should I be saving?

The short answer: most probably more than you are at the moment and as much as you can. We live in uncertain times when, unfortunately, our jobs are easily lost, our incomes are fragile and we can't rely on the state to provide anything other than a basic financial safety net.

We are also living longer, with retirements of 20 to 30 years becoming increasingly common. Sadly, there is more chance that Elton John will be caught in the arms of a beautiful woman than there is that the government will provide you with a comfortable retirement, while many employers have been cutting back on the pension deals they're offering their staff.

The good news? You've got a long life ahead of you. The bad news? You're going to have to save more to pay for it, grandma. A study from Scottish Widows, a pension-fund manager, found that we'd apparently like an income of £30,000 a year to enjoy when we retire and yet unsurprisingly only one in twelve of us is actually saving enough money to hit that target. 'The truth of the matter is quite simple,' reckons a guy in a suit at Scottish Widows. 'If you want to have a fairly comfortable retirement you should be saving at least 12% of your earnings year in, year out from the age of 30 until retirement at 65.'

In fact, another study by the Association of British Insurers found that almost 8 million of us are not saving anything at all for our retirements – with 25- to 29-year-olds the most guilty – while another 4 million of us are saving only very diddy amounts.

But if you haven't started yet it's not too late – it just means you'll have to save a little bit more. A nice rule of thumb is to halve your age (no cheating, now, ladies), put a percentage sign at the end and put that much of your gross annual salary towards your retirement each year.

So if you are twenty you should be putting 10% of your gross annual salary into a pension each year and if you are forty you should be putting in 20%. By the way, gross doesn't mean your annual salary makes you want to puke – it's the amount you're paid before the government puts on its hoody and robs you of tax.

And it's not just your retirement you need to save for. The housing boom has meant that it has become increasingly difficult to get on the property ladder without a substantial deposit. In fact, a 5% deposit will set you back a whopping £8,042 based on the price of the average UK house. And if it's your first car you're after? That'll be £3,400. A wedding, including honeymoon, will strip you of £15,764, and a three-year university course for your kid, outside London, with living expenses included, will hit you for £23,150.

On top of this, you should also have at least three times and preferably six times your monthly take-home pay stashed away in an instant-access savings account to cover any life-changing circumstances, such as unemployment or illness.

And the trick with all this is to start early. Why? Because the beauty of compound interest means the sooner you begin saving the more money you'll make.

Compound what?

If there's any magic when it comes to saving, the power of compound interest is it. When you put money away, your Fat Belly bank adds interest to your savings at regular intervals. If you don't touch the interest and combine it to your initial lump sum you then start to earn interest on your interest, as well as on the original amount you saved.

For example, if the annual interest rate is 5% you will earn £5 interest over the course of a year on a £100 deposit. If you save another £100 the next year you will get interest on this as well as the £105 you had from the previous year. Earning interest on your interest is the miracle of compounding.

It's very much like a snowball effect. As your initial lump sum rolls down the side of the mountain it gets bigger and bigger. Even if you start with a small snowball, given enough time, you can end up with one large enough to do some serious damage to the side of your Chubby bank's head.

And the earlier you start investing the better. Someone who invests £100 a month for just nine years from the age of 20 and then lets their investments grow is likely to have more money at the age of 60 than someone who invests £100 a month for 30 years after their 30th birthday. In fact, if you save £100 a month for 40 years and your investments compound at 6.5% a year you'll amass yourself a mighty pot of £218,107. A lot of wonga.

But the rate your Fat Belly bank offers you is equally as important as the length of time you invest for. There's no point tucking your money away for years on end in an account that pays less than 1% interest a year – some of the high-street banks offer accounts that pay as little interest as 0.1% – when the best deal on the market is much, much higher.

Get out of the habit of opening an account, depositing your cash each month and then forgetting about it. The rate your Chubby bank offers you is crucial to the miracle of compound interest, and so you need to keep an eye out for which one is peddling the best rates. Another rule of thumb is that, before tax, your savings should earn at least the Bank of England's base rate, which at the time of writing is 5.25%. But by expending only a little energy, such as getting online and checking out the best-buy tables in the national newspapers, you should be able to beat the base rate with your eyes closed. (Actually, keep them open until you've read the tables.)

If you stuffed £100 a month under your mattress, down your pants or under the floorboards you would have £24,000 after twenty years. All you'd get back is the money you saved, absolutely no interest and a bulging pair of pants (not so bad if you're a fella). If you paid £100 a month into an account that offered just 1% you'd get an extra £2,566 back after 20 years while an account that paid 5% a year would return you a whopping £40,754.

You need to shop around and treat your savings in the same way you would any other purchase. If you were buying a TV you would ask your mates if they knew which ones were the best, buy a specialist magazine to find out the ones it rated the most or go online to get some advice. The same principles need to be applied when it comes to your savings.

There are thousands of savings products on offer from hundreds of different financial companies. But, unless you go for one of the market's better rates, you might find that inflation has eaten into your savings and left them a lot less plumper than you thought.

The Jargonator: Base rate

The interest rate set by the Bank of England, used as a basis for the rates that the Fat Belly banks offer their customers. The base rate can go down as well as up.

Inflation? What are you talking about inflation for?

OK, relax. Inflation is one of those words that make people's eyes glaze over and have them running for the door. But inflation is very easy to understand and very crucial to your savings, so take your trainers off and bear with me for a moment or two.

First, all inflation refers to is the general increase in prices. Over the last five years inflation in the UK has grown by 1.7% each year on average, meaning that it now costs you £1.99 to buy a Big Mac instead of £1.83, or £3 to buy a pint of beer instead of £2.75.

The danger when it comes to your savings is that, unless the rate of interest your Fat Belly bank pays you is greater than or at least equal to the rate of inflation, you'll be able to buy fewer Big Macs or a smaller round of drinks when you come to spend your cash.

For example, if you have £1,000 in a current account with one of the many high-street banks that pay next to nothing in interest each year (for the sake of argument we'll assume it's zero) and inflation goes up by 2.5% a year, then your £1,000 will be worth just £884 in five years' time and only £610 in twenty years' time. Your £1,000 will still be £1,000 but it will have been frozen in time while the price of everything else has gone up.

In simple terms, you must find yourself a savings account that pays you at least (and preferably much more than) the annual rate of inflation. And, for your peace of mind, all of the accounts listed in the best-buy savings tables will do that.

What about tax?

Good question. Not only do you need to find an inflation-proof savings rate, but you also need to find a rate that is taxproof. If you're a basic-rate taxpayer and pay capital-gains tax at a rate of 20%, a 5% return on your savings will be worth 4%, i.e. 20% less. That's because as well as income tax, inheritance tax and value-added tax, you unfortunately also have to pay tax on the interest you earn and so you need to factor this into your calculations when choosing an account.

So if you earn the average wage and pay capital-gains tax at 20%, the 5% rate your Chubby bank is advertising will be worth only 4%. At the same time, if the UK's rate of inflation is running at 2.5%, the real rate of return on your savings will fall to 1.5% (4% minus 2.5%). Not as attractive as you first thought, but at least your savings are now inflation- and taxproof, meaning you won't have to scrimp on the Big Macs.

Saving not investing

Saving and investing are two very similar terms that are
sometimes interchanged and often confused. Quite simply,
however, saving refers to the process of sticking your money
away in very low-risk products, such as a high-street or
Internet savings account, where you get back at least what you
put in with some interest on top. The idea is that your money
is completely safe. There are some risks, of course. The bank
you invest in could collapse and unless you choose an account
with a competitive rate of interest there is a chance your
savings will be gobbled up by rising inflation. But these risks
are small and easily managed.

The process of investing, on the other hand, assumes you
are prepared to lose some or all of your original investment in
the hope that it will grow into something bigger. Investing in
shares or bonds, for example, implies you are happy to take
more risk with your money and are prepared – but hopefully
this won't happen – to get back less than you put in. Never
invest in any particular product unless you are prepared to lose
what you put in. If you have £5,000 at your disposal, which you
want to use as a deposit on a house or flat in a few months'
time, don't put it at risk. Instead tuck it away in a savings
account that offers one of the market's best rates of interest.
If you have a sum of money that you don't need immediate
access to or you have money left over each month that you're
prepared to take a risk with, then by all means invest it. Just
always remind yourself that you could lose it. If that's a bitter
pill to swallow, stick to saving.

The expert view: How much should I be stashing away?

Mark Taylor, director of savings, investments and pensions at Virgin Money

Savings, for most of us, revolve around life events: retirement, a deposit for a house or putting kids through university. Getting into the habit of saving means you will be better prepared to realise that event when it arrives.

Before thinking about saving, ensure you have no short-term debts such as credit cards or loans. Some think it is OK to save with outstanding debts on a credit card, but there is no sense in doing this if the rate of interest you pay on a credit card outstrips the interest you earn on a deposit account.

Next, make a budget and decide how much you can afford to save each month. Set up a direct debit and stick with your plan. How much you can afford to put away will vary, but 15% of your monthly salary is a good target to aim for.

When you first start to save, open an instant-access deposit account. The account should enable you to get at your savings quickly should the need arise.

Each year you can put up to £3,000 (set to rise to £3,600 by April 2008) into a cash ISA (a form of deposit account). This means you earn tax-free interest, saving you hundreds of pounds over the long term. Always ensure you make use of your tax allowances first when saving.

Shop around for the best savings deals. Some accounts have restrictions and variable interest rates according to the amount you save. When starting out, look for an account that pays a good rate of interest, irrespective of how much you invest. Even better, look for a guarantee that the interest rate will never fall below, say, 1% of the Bank of England rate. This saves you having to shop around when rates move.

Andrew Jones, director of savings at Barclays

Despite living in a more attractive saving environment due to the recent Bank of England interest-rate increases, the average amount we put away is not enough with many of us having less than £3,000 in savings. We could be left with a shortfall if we have to give up work or lose our jobs unexpectedly.

Of course, it's easy to put off saving for the unexpected as the cost of living has increased by 16% on average over the last decade with some everyday items substantially higher than the average. For example, electricity, gas and other fuels have increased by 52%, package holidays by 49%, eating out by 35% and rent by 32%. But there are a few areas that have fallen in price in the last decade: household appliances have fallen by 28%, clothing by 45% and cars by 12%.

Putting all these things to one side, you should be setting aside the equivalent of three months' salary for unforeseen life events. This may seem like an awful lot of money but it will ensure you have a financial cushion while you get back on your feet. So if you are earning the national average £25,000 you should have at least £4,653 stashed away.

If you have debts it's worthwhile looking to reduce them in the most cost-effective way by consolidating and opting for 0% deals. By doing this you can structure the debt without paying interest and may still have the opportunity to put something away for unforeseen situations.

It's also worth reviewing your monthly expenditure to reduce outgoings on bills such as gas and electricity and it is certainly essential to look at your biggest financial commitments, such as your mortgage. Thousands of people with mortgages could easily save 25% a year, which could be reinvested in some form of savings. A person with a £100,000 mortgage, for example, could save as much as £1,700 a year.

Don't just bank on it: finding the right current account

Right, let's get this straight from the outset. If you have money in a current account – and I know that six out of seven of you do – then you should be looking to get as much interest on that money as you possibly can.

Yes, I know current accounts are designed to give you easy access to your money and that they're more about getting your cash out rather than putting it in, but that doesn't mean you have to tolerate dismal rates of return on the money you keep in there.

Current accounts can be a very important savings device. In fact some will pay you a higher rate of interest than many specialist savings accounts, which don't allow you immediate access to your dough.

The trouble is that we have been brainwashed into thinking it's OK to accept derisory rates of interest on our current accounts. The big four high-street banks – Barclays, HSBC, Lloyds TSB and (RBS) NatWest – control roughly 70% of all current accounts and have only ever offered us rates at bitterly low levels. Levels so small and laughable even Danny DeVito would be jealous.

We have been conditioned into thinking we can't demand a current account with attractive rates of interest, but that's nonsense. The advent of online banking and the emergence of new financial providers have meant you can now open a current account that pays at least fifty times more interest than the 0.1% rate you've grown accustomed to.

The introduction of a new generation of current accounts means you're now able to tuck into interest rates in excess of 5%. You might not get as fat as the Chubby banks but you no longer need to starve on measly portions of interest. The time has come to have your cake and eat it, my friends.

What is a current account?

Unlike that in a savings account, the money you hold in a current account can be withdrawn immediately. Current accounts offer a safe place to store your day-to-day money, and you will be given a chequebook and a debit card or cash card to get at your money as easily and quickly as possible. Some will also offer overdraft facilities, enabling you to borrow if it ever becomes necessary. Current accounts have also distinguished themselves from savings accounts by the paltry level of interest they've traditionally offered. The advent of online banking and the emergence of increased levels of competition, however, have meant this is no longer the case. The line of distinction has been blurred with some current accounts offering better rates of interest than some savings accounts.

But what's stopping me?

Loyalty. Loyalty is admirable in every other aspect of life except when it comes to your savings. Your Fat Belly bank loves the fact you are loyal and that is the reason he is paying you peanuts on the balance in your current account. He thinks you're a monkey.

I'll say this once more, but it's the final time. You are more likely to leave your partner than you are your bank, so listen up.

According to a study by Abbey, the high-street bank, almost two-thirds of us stay with the same provider because we think transferring our direct debits and standing orders to another bank would be too much hassle. Another 25% of us stay put because we assume the Fat Belly banks won't help us to switch, while almost 50% of us don't move because we think all banks are the same. Tosh. Moving to a bank that pays 5% on balances up to £2,500 will net you £125 over the course of a year compared with the £2.50 a Chubby bank will give you at a rate of 0.1%. You may well feel more secure with your bank but do you really want to forgo more than £100 a year for that feeling?

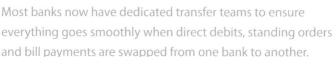

The transfer process

Most banks now have dedicated transfer teams to ensure everything goes smoothly when direct debits, standing orders and bill payments are swapped from one bank to another.

The physical transfer process should take less than a week to complete. However, it is best to pick a point in the month when there is minimal account activity to help ensure the process runs as smoothly as possible. It is also advisable to ask for a single person (a point of contact, not an unmarried person, Romeo) whom you can get hold of at the bank while the transfer is taking place.

Also, for those worried about damaging their credit rating, such as those applying for a mortgage or personal loan, the timing of any account switch may need some thought. A lot of lenders give points to people who have held an account with the same institution for a number of years and if you switch accounts just as you apply for a mortgage you might get marked down.

Is there anything I need to watch out for?

Yes. The first thing you need to be wary of before you jump ship is whether the interest rates on offer are exactly what they seem. A number of bank accounts boast fantastic rates of interest but only if you meet certain conditions.

For example, some Chubby banks will offer you rates above and beyond 5% but only if you pay in at least £1,000 per month. Pay in less than that and you'll earn rates below 1% and that is often inclusive of an introductory bonus.

Also remember that many of the headline-grabbing interest rates may stay headline-grabbing only for a set period. Many deals come to market fattened up with introductory bonuses, which run out after six or nine months. After this, your rate could drop considerably or it may start to track the Bank of England's base rate, which can go up or down.

At the same time, some providers will offer attractive rates only up to certain savings limits, such as £2,500 or £5,000. Go over those ceilings and the rate offered could fall to as little as 0.1% on the excess.

Also, keep a close eye on your interest rate by checking it at least three or four times a year. Banks love launching headline-grabbing accounts, raking in new customers and then putting those accounts on the back burner. The Fat Belly banks then start cutting the interest rates on these dormant or non-marketed accounts and unless you're vigilant you may find your once fantastic rate of interest has disappeared before your very eyes.

In general, the better the rate is, the more conditions you'll probably have to meet. You may find that you have to make a minimum number of transactions each month or, if you choose an online bank, you may be required to log on a minimum number of times a month to get the advertised rate. The solution? Be aware that these conditions exist and make sure you know about the ones that apply to your account.

'As the number and variety of accounts increases, so seems their complexity,' says Rachel Thrussell, head of savings research at Moneyfacts, the independent money-data provider. 'Many accounts now offer introductory bonuses, rate guarantees, tiered rates, restrictions on the number of withdrawals and a whole array of conditions. But it is well worthwhile for consumers to shop around to secure a good home for their hard-earned cash. Taking, for example, a deposit of £5,000, an additional 2% interest would earn an extra £100 year – not a bad return for a few minutes' work.'

Don't forget your overdraft

The advice in this section is geared towards your moving to another provider based on the interest it offers on account balances. But if more often than not you are overdrawn rather than in credit there is no point concentrating on credit interest rates. Going for an account that offers a credit interest rate of 5% is pointless if you are permanently overdrawn and the overdraft rate you are being hit with is in the region of 20%. Instead, switch to one of the many accounts plugging an introductory overdraft rate of 0% for a fixed period or a permanently low rate. If you only *sometimes* slip into the red, you should go for a high-interest account, which comes with an interest-free buffer overdraft of between £100 and £500. Even if your current account is always in credit, it is never a bad idea to arrange a small overdraft limit just in case.

What else should I keep my eyes peeled for?

Yes, you also need to watch out for fees. First Direct, the online arm of HSBC, bucked the trend of offering fee-free current accounts by charging customers £120 a year if they do not pay at least £1,500 a month into their accounts or keep an average monthly balance of £1,500. The bank also said it would waive fees if customers took out another one of their products, such as a savings account, credit card, personal loan, mortgage or home insurance.

But these fees are unacceptable and should be avoided. Several banks charge up to £15 a month for packaged or premium current accounts, which come with perks such as free travel insurance or cut-price currency exchange, but First Direct's £10 monthly charge comes with no such frills.

First Direct may well have paved the way for other banks to follow suit and start applying charges to their basic current accounts but at the time of writing no other provider has done so. So the solution is very easy: avoid current accounts that charge a fee and switch to one of the many that don't. If your Chubby bank begins charging you a tenner a month for nothing, it's time to get your coat.

Packaged accounts: are they worth it?

Your conversation might have gone a little something like this. 'By the way, Mr Newlands, just before you go, my records show that as one of our most valued customers you have the option of upgrading your account to our Privilege Gold Plus account, which will allow you to take advantage of a number of free additional services, such as travel insurance, car-breakdown cover, mobile-phone insurance and card protection. There's a small monthly charge for this service but as a Privilege Gold Plus member ... blah, blah, blah.'

Before you knew it your head had swollen to the size of a watermelon, you thought you were richer than Richard Branson and you signed up to an account with a number of 'free' additional services you have still yet to use. Does that sound familiar?

According to a report from uSwitch, the price-comparison website, one in nine current-account holders – some 4.5 million of us – has been 'upgraded' to a packaged account on the advice of a Fat Belly bank. We pay an average £10 a month for the privilege and yet more than one in four of us never bother to use the 'free' perks on offer. To add insult to injury, the bulk of these accounts, despite being promoted as premium or upmarket products, pay interest on credit balances lower than 1%. Of course, free insurance and breakdown cover can be worthwhile but you need to check the details carefully – for instance, many of these free travel policies will cover joint account holders only if they're travelling together, not separately. Also much of what you've been offered may well be covered by your existing household insurance.

And remember: you're paying £120 a year for this 'free' cover. Depending on your needs, breakdown cover can cost two-thirds less, while an annual European travel policy could cost you around £50.

Unless you can really make good use of the benefits offered, avoid fee-paying accounts and go for one that simply pays a decent interest rate. Keep your ego in check and don't fall for the sales pitch.

Get into the Internet

When it comes to getting one of the market's best current-account rates, the online banks are your friends. Whether it's because they pay less for building space, employ fewer staff or have lower energy bills, the online providers seem to offer better rates of interest than their bricks-and-mortar cousins.

They may have funny-sounding names, such as Smile, Cahoot, Virgin Money and Egg, but that doesn't mean you shouldn't take them seriously. Around 42 million of us will bank online by 2020, according to a survey carried out by Alliance & Leicester, but people still shy away from Internet providers because they don't have recognisable names. More often than not, however, these online banks are owned by well-known high-street firms. For example, Cahoot is an offshoot of Abbey, Smile is a part of the Co-operative Bank, First Direct is owned by HSBC and Egg was laid by Prudential.

Try to get over your fear of banking online – but do always keep your wits about you. Online banking fraud has shot up by more than 8,000% over the last two years, according to the Financial Services Authority. Indeed, some reports show that we fear Internet crime more than being burgled.

If you are thinking about banking online, or you already do, here are a few pointers to help keep you fraud-free.

- **Never respond to an email from your bank asking you either to send or enter your account details at a website. You are being scammed. Your bank will never ask you to email personal details, so don't.**
- **Never access your account from unknown PCs, such as those found at Internet cafés or libraries. They are often targeted by fraudsters and can be riddled with programs designed to make off with your personal information.**
- **Check your computer for spyware. These programs, once installed, are capable of gathering up email addresses, passwords and credit-card numbers and then transmitting them to someone somewhere else.**
- **Never log on without first installing a firewall. If anyone or anything tries to access your PC from the outside or, more worryingly, any unauthorised internal software tries to send information out, your firewall will alert you and ask you if it needs to be blocked.**
- **Install antivirus protection. Without a decent antivirus package, your PC will come under attack as soon as you connect to the Internet and, in no time, it will become a magnet for harmful programs.**
- **Never use the word password as your password. Nearly half of us do, making the online thief's life even easier.**

Casebook: The unwanted package

Dominic De Terville, 32, from south London

I already had quite a large overdraft with my bank and because I was about to move into a new flat I needed to club together six weeks' worth of rent to give to my landlord as a deposit. I approached my bank to see if they could help me out by extending my overdraft to £3,500 and they said they could but only if I upgraded my account to one of their premier offerings.

The person I spoke to at the bank gave me all the spin that not everyone was allowed to upgrade and that it was an option for me only because I was a valued and loyal customer. But flattery had nothing to do with why I went for the packaged account they were offering. The real clincher was that the overdraft rate on the upgraded account was ten percentage points lower than the rate on my old account.

The new rate was going to save me a lot of money each month despite the fact the account carried a charge of £250 a year. The fee worried me but it still worked out cheaper for me as I used my overdraft a lot and there were a lot of extra benefits on the account. I also needed the money for the deposit fairly quickly and so it seemed like a good option. I thought it would be only a temporary measure, anyway.

But three years on I still have the upgraded account and have paid £750 for the privilege. What's more I've never once used any of the free benefits the account offers.

It bothers me that I have paid out so much money to them, as they generally haven't treated me well over the years, particularly while I was a student. I've thought about leaving many times but I guess I've just been too lazy. This year, however, it's on the list of things I need to do.

Casebook: The dropper and swapper

Lynn Tildesly, 40, from Manchester

I had been with my bank, NatWest, since I was sixteen and was perfectly happy until I got talked into upgrading my account to one of its premier offerings. Basically, I felt as if I had been bamboozled into signing up for a £10-a-month account I didn't want with lots of extras I didn't use.

Not only was I not using the freebies, such as travel insurance, but the account paid next to nothing in interest and I was constantly being called at home by a personal banker to ask me if there was anything I needed. I asked NatWest if I could swap back to my old account but they seemed reluctant to do so, so I decided to change banks completely.

Having asked some of my friends and having looked at a few of the best-buy tables on the Internet, I decided to swap to First Direct, which had a good reputation and offered a decent interest rate on account balances. The move was completely trouble-free and First Direct swapped over all my direct debits and standing orders with no hassle.

The problem, however, is that not long after I moved First Direct introduced a £10 monthly charge on its basic account. Luckily, I'd opened a savings account at the same time, which made me exempt from any charges, but I fear I might have to pay a fee at some point down the line and want to get out. Had First Direct told me that they were thinking about introducing fees at the time I signed up I would never have joined.

Because I now know how easy it is to swap banks I'm not worried about moving for a second time – I would rather not, but it doesn't now seem like such a hassle. I haven't moved yet, as I want to first find out a little bit more about offset accounts, which group together your savings with your mortgage, but I will be moving soon.

Know your ISA from your elbow

Can you remember the first time someone asked you if you had an ISA? I can, and it made me feel slightly nauseous. I mean, what the hell was an ISA? It was early in the morning and I definitely had bad breath, a stinking headache and sticky-up hair but I couldn't recall having an ISA – so I just said no.

A few days later one of my mates said he'd opened an ISA and that I should do the same. I shuffled my feet, kept my eyes glued to the floor and said I definitely would. Then, to rub salt in my already ignorant wounds, my mum – that's right, my mum – phoned me to inform me she'd got herself an ISA and that she couldn't have been happier.

I felt alone – what were these bloody ISAs and why didn't I have one? Those three little letters had me in a panic, so I popped round to my mum's and asked her to spill the beans. She took off her apron, put down her rolling pin and said, 'Oh, they're just a tax-free shelter for your savings.'

The point I'm rather clumsily trying to make is that an ISA – like the offside rule – is one of those things that sound really difficult and scary but are actually very simple. In fact, the key thing to remember when it comes to ISAs is that they are your friends.

OK – so what are they?

First, *ISA* is short for *individual savings account* and, as my mum so succinctly put it, they are a tax-free way both to save and to invest your money. They are not a savings product in themselves, such as a postal account or a fixed-rate savings account, but a kind of overcoat that you can wrap around the shoulders of your fixed-rate savings account to protect it from the taxman's thieving hands.

As a taxpayer, you normally have to pay tax on any interest you earn from the money you've tucked away in a standard bank or building-society savings account. The tax is deducted from the interest before it is paid out to you, reducing the amount you get. Likewise, you have to pay tax on all the profits you make if you invest your dough in the stock market. An ISA, however, allows you to put money away each year into a range of savings and investments products and pay no tax at all on the profits.

The power of the cash ISA in numbers

The full £3,000 allowance (which is set to rise to £3,600 by April 2008) invested in a top-paying cash ISA, such as a 5.55% account, would earn you £166.50 a year in interest. A basic-rate taxpayer therefore saves £33.30 in tax, which would have been deducted at source, while a higher-rate taxpayer saves £66.50. With the beauty of compound interest, and assuming that £3,000 is invested every year for the next ten years at the same rate of interest, the account will grow to almost £41,000. Now, had you put that money in a regular savings account paying the same rate of interest a basic-rate taxpayer would have lost £2,173 and a higher-rate taxpayer nearly £4,500.

So why can't I invest all my money in an ISA?

Because the government has set limits on how much of your money you can wrap your ISA overcoat around. The government introduced ISAs in 1999 to try to encourage us to put more money away and to mould us into a nation of savers rather than a nation of borrowers. But they weren't about to lose their minds and allow you to save and invest everything tax-free.

Noooooooo! What they said was that you could save up to £7,000 a year, increasing to £7,200 in April 2008, into some sort of saving or investment product, wrap your ISA overcoat around it, and not pay a penny in tax on the income you get from your investment. For everything over and above £7,000 the government would still be able to don its hoody and rob you of tax in the way it always has.

The lowdown

Up until April 2007, ISAs have come in two forms: a mini ISA, with an annual limit of £3,000 for cash or £4,000 for stocks and shares; and a maxi ISA, with an annual limit of £7,000 as long as you haven't touched your mini allowance.

The idea behind this rather complicated setup was that, if you wanted to invest in both cash and the stock market, you had to take out two mini ISAs with different specialist providers, or if you wanted to maximise your exposure to the stock market you could buy a single maxi wrapper. You couldn't, however, take out a mini and a maxi ISA in the same tax year.

But in a welcome drive for simplification the government announced that the mini/maxi distinction would be scrapped, so that there will just be cash ISAs and stocks and shares ISAs, not mini and maxi ones. You can invest in one of each every tax year, which runs from 6 April to 5 April, and split your £7,000 limit between them – as long as the cash part does not exceed £3,000.

Previously, if you had invested in a cash ISA at a Fat Belly bank (because it had the best market rates) and then noticed the interest on your account had fallen, maybe because an introductory bonus period had finished, you would have been allowed to switch your money only into another cash ISA. Under the new guidelines, however, you can now also switch your money into a stocks-and-shares ISA and still hold on to your tax-free allowance.

The idea behind this is to enable those of us who have built up sufficient precautionary savings in cash ISAs – and there is more than £190 billion of our money stashed away in these tax-free babies – to have the freedom to invest that money in the potentially higher returning stock market.

The economic secretary to the Treasury says, 'Our aim is to further promote share ownership by encouraging savers to diversify their assets and benefit from the potentially higher returns offered by stocks and shares over the long run.'

The government also announced that ISAs are to be made a permanent feature of the savings landscape. When they were introduced in 1999 they were originally due to last for just ten years, but some 16 million ISA accounts have since been opened and bags of money has been tucked away in them.

'Our task is to entrench a culture of savings for people of all ages,' adds the same economic secretary. 'This largest ever reform to the ISA regime will simplify personal savings and help more families to save for their future, ensuring that everyone can share in rising prosperity. This open-ended commitment to the ISA will provide stability for savers.'

But I don't pay tax

If you are a non-taxpayer and you don't earn enough to pay income tax, you won't necessarily get the best rates by putting your money into a cash ISA. This is because, as a non-taxpayer, you can register to get your interest paid gross, without the tax being deducted, on any bank or building society account of your choice. You should scour all of the best-buy savings tables, not just the ones for cash ISAs, and pick the best one. To register for gross interest all you need to do is fill out an R85 form, which will be available at your chosen bank or building society as well as your local tax office.

So what does this all mean for me?

Well, when it comes to putting money away in a low-risk savings account, a hell of a lot. Tucking money away in a cash ISA should be the first move for any taxpayer wanting to maximise the interest they get on their savings.

The reason is simple. Basic-rate taxpayers pay tax at 20% and higher-rate taxpayers pay tax at 40%. That means that, for every £100 of interest earned, you'd receive the whole amount in a cash ISA but only £80 in a normal savings account if you were a basic-rate taxpayers. Higher-rate taxpayers would get just £60.

In other words the best-paying savings account would have to give you 20 or 40% more interest each year than the best-paying cash ISA just to keep your pockets lined in the same way. But, let me assure you, they don't. In fact, at the time of writing, the best-paying no-notice savings account returned roughly a quarter of 1% less than the best cash ISA.

The golden rule: stick your money in a top-paying cash ISA first. Once you've reached your yearly tax-free savings limit, put the remainder in the best-paying regular savings account. Do it the other way round and I'll be forced to give you a beating.

Dispelling the myths about cash ISAs

Your money needs to be invested for a certain length of time before it becomes tax-free. Rubbish! Unlike the case with TESSAs, the tax-exempt saving scheme that ISAs replaced, money can be withdrawn from an ISA at any time without implicating your tax position. If you have chosen a cash ISA that requires thirty days' notice to get to your money, for example, then you will have to wait thirty days, but that has nothing to do with your tax position.

You have to be over eighteen to save money in an ISA. Not exactly. It's true you have to be over eighteen to invest in a stocks-and-shares ISA but, to put money away in a cash ISA, sixteen is the magic number.

You can withdraw money you've saved from previous tax years, put it in another cash ISA and it'll still be safe from taxman. No. If you've saved your full tax allowance with one Fat Belly bank for three years and want to switch that £9,000 (plus all that interest you've earned) to another Chubby bank offering a higher rate of interest, organise that switch via your bank. Do not just take the money out yourself. If you do, your £9,000 will no longer be sheltered from the taxman.

You can save your full tax allowance in one year, take out some of that money and still reinvest it during the same tax year. Wrong. If you put £3,000 into a cash ISA and then withdraw £1,000, you will not be allowed to replace that £1,000 until the following year.

You need to be rich to invest in a cash ISA. Nonsense! Many of the cash ISAs on the market require you to make an initial payment of just £1. There are some accounts that require you to invest your full cash ISA limit in one go but, if you don't have that, simply avoid them.

What to watch out for

In general, the better the rate is, the more conditions you'll probably have to meet. Cash ISA providers play the same games as savings- and current-account providers, so you need to be on your toes. For example, one cash ISA might include a short-term bonus and have annual limits on withdrawals, while another might include a transfer penalty – which means you will be hit with a charge if you switch to another cash ISA.

The trouble is that you have to be extra vigilant when it comes to cash ISAs because, unlike other best-buy savings tables, the best cash ISAs are all just lumped together. For other regular accounts you may have a separate table for Internet banks, a separate table for instant-access accounts and a separate table for fixed-rate accounts. But for cash ISAs no such distinctions are made.

Which means you might come across a table that looks a little something like this:

Cash ISAs

Lender	Account	Notice or term	Minimum deposit £	Rate %	Interest paid
Fat Belly bank	30-day-notice ISA	30 days	3,000	5.85*	Y
Chubby bank	Tracker ISA	15 days (P)	1,000	5.80*	Y
Big-Boned bank	Direct ISA	None (I)	10	5.55	Y
Podgy bank	Premier ISA	None	1	5.45	Y

As you can see, Fat Belly bank's cash ISA is top of the charts with a rate of 5.85%. It betters Chubby bank's deal by 0.05% and beats Big-Boned bank's rate by 0.3%. But it comes with a lot of catches.

First and foremost, you need to have at least £3,000 ready to put away. If you haven't got that much, then cross it off your list. A more suitable option if you've got less than £3,000 but more than a tenner is Big-Boned's Direct ISA. But this doesn't come without its complications, either.

For a start it doesn't pay as much as Fat Belly's deal and secondly the *I* in parentheses means it's an Internet account. If you don't have the Internet at home or are not allowed to use it at work for personal use, then it might be best to stay clear of this account and go for Podgy bank's deal, which doesn't come with any hidden surprises, just a rate that is 0.4% lower than Fat Belly's.

If you do have £3,000 ready to go, then there are a couple more things to take into consideration before you hand over your cash to either Fat Belly or Chubby bank. The first thing is that your money cannot be immediately withdrawn from either account. Fat Belly requires thirty days' notice before it'll give you your money and Chubby needs fifteen days.

Also the asterisks next to both banks' rates means they have included an introductory bonus in their headline rate, which will run out after a certain period of time, usually six months. The tables often don't tell you how much the bonus is, just that it is there. Typically, however, it's in the region of half of 1%.

The *P* in parentheses in Big-Boned bank's deal means it is a postal account. And the *Y* you can see marked against all the deals means that the interest is paid yearly as opposed to monthly.

Fortune favours the very organised

For the extra savvy and well organised of you out there you could actually make a small pot of dough from the high rates cash ISAs offer and the 0% rates some credit-card providers are peddling.

The idea is simple, really. Open up a credit card with a 0% rate that remains at 0% for as long as possible, ideally twelve months, have your credit limit – preferably the full cash ISA limit – transferred to your current account and then shove that money into the best-paying cash ISA.

Having £3,000 tucked away in a cash ISA at a rate of 5% – which is considerably lower than the best rates currently on offer – would return you £150 over the course of a year or £12.50 a month.

To make this work, however, you need to switch out of your 0% rate and into another 0% card before your card's non-introductory rate kicks in.

Remember, though, that the majority of credit-card firms – but not all – now slap on a balance-transfer fee for moving your balance to one of their rivals. That means that shifting your debt of £3,000 between two companies would cost you £90 if the transfer fee is 3%.

But that still leaves you with a profit of £90 and you may even be able to swap to a card that will give you another £3,600 on top of your original £3,000 to put into your cash ISA the following year.

With the beauty of compound interest, that means you'll get a return of £355 on your £6,750 if the rate on your account stays at the same 5%. Not bad, not bad at all.

Adding more juice: savings accounts

Right, before we get started adding more juice, there are two things you should have sorted out by now: your current account and a cash ISA.

By now you'll know very well that you don't have to put up with measly rates of interest on your current account. A lot of the Fat Belly banks pay 0.1% interest on our account balances but some of the best providers offer at least fifty times more.

If your Chubby bank is treating you like a monkey and paying you peanuts it's time to get angry. Put the book down, have a look at a few of the current-account best-buy tables on the Internet and say goodbye to Chubby. It's easy. Your new provider will transfer all of your direct debits and standing orders for you.

Remember, there's nothing current about your account if you're being paid interest of 0.1%.

Secondly, forget about putting your hard-earned cash into a top-paying savings account unless you've already squeezed the last penny out of your yearly tax-free allowance. If you pay tax and you have savings get a cash ISA first.

Why? Because basic-rate taxpayers pay tax at 20% and higher-rate taxpayers pay tax at 40%. And that means you would have to get 20 or 40% more interest each year from the best-paying savings account to beat the best-paying cash ISA – but you won't. Fill up on a cash ISA before you do anything else.

Now you're ready to examine your other savings account options.

Option 1: Easy-access savings accounts

As the name would suggest, an easy-access or no-notice savings account lets you get hold of your cash at short notice, usually within a few days. Notice accounts, on the other hand, may deny you access to your money for a period of up to thirty, sixty or ninety days – so, if you need to get to your dough quickly, you need a no-notice account.

Although current accounts may sometimes pay the same interest as or even more than easy-access savings accounts, having a separate account in which to store your money will make it easier for you to tuck money away and keep track of your savings.

For starters, you can set up a monthly standing order from your current account to your savings account on the day you get paid, which will not only simplify the savings process but also help you get into the routine of putting money aside. If you leave your savings to slosh around in your current account you make it difficult to assess what you've already put away and, more critically, you might spend it.

But, as with all things financial, you need to keep your eyes peeled for any catches. One annoying trick that the Fat Belly banks have started pulling is to charge you a penalty to get at your cash immediately.

Traditionally, the point of an instant-access account was to withdraw your money quickly without penalties. That also traditionally meant that the interest rates on these accounts were not overly generous. But that is no longer the case. With the exception of some of the branch-based high-street accounts, no-notice accounts now pay some of the market's highest rates.

The trade-off, however, has been the introduction of charges. You can still get your money out instantly but you may have to pay a fee to do so, such as forgoing a month's worth of interest.

'Within the traditional definition of an instant-access savings account, the concept of incurring a penalty for withdrawals would be a contradiction in terms,' says Rachel Thrussell at Moneyfacts, the independent money-data provider. 'Usually, if we choose an instant-access account to house our savings, it is because we are happy to forsake the highest rates of return for immediate access to our money – with the rate guaranteed to be paid regardless of the number of withdrawals made.'

Another trick is for the Chubby banks to include a bonus rate on their no-notice account, which runs out after the first six months. This will typically be in the region of 0.5% and will push the account higher up the best-buy tables and make deals seem more attractive than they actually are.

For the very proactive of you out there, these bonuses don't need to present a problem. As soon as your bonus runs out, shift your money into a better-paying account. Easy. Remember, though, that your Chubby bank is not obliged to tell you when your bonus is about to end, so you need to be on your toes.

If, however, changing accounts is not for you – and, let's face it, for many people it's not: as I've said, I have friends who have enough trouble changing their pants – then you might want to go for a high-paying account that guarantees to match or beat the Bank of England's base rate for a set period. One such example is the Icesave account, launched by Landsbanki, which guarantees to beat UK base rates by at least 0.25% until October 2009.

Also, when you're choosing accounts make sure you're always comparing like with like. Banks quote one of two different rates when advertising their deals: the gross rate or the annual equivalent rate (AER). The gross rate is the flat amount paid; the AER takes into account interest compounded over the year. If a deal has a six-month bonus, the AER is a good way to compare it with other deals, because it calculates the average rate of interest you receive over the whole year (i.e. six months with a bonus and six months without), not just the rate you are given on day one. AER is a more accurate way to compare rates.

Option 2: Notice accounts

A notice account lets you get hold of your money only after a specified period, such as thirty, sixty or ninety days. If you don't give sufficient notice, you're going to be hit with a penalty equal to the interest payable during that notice period

It used to be that notice accounts offered the market's best rates of interest, but that is often no longer the case. The launch of post, phone and Internet accounts, where *you* do most of the work, has meant that instant-access accounts offer rates that are as competitive as, if not better than, those of notice accounts. But that doesn't mean they don't have their plus points.

If you're an impulse buyer and you tend to spend all of the money you have access to, then a notice account might be a good option for you. You can look at it as a pair of handcuffs.

Having to wait up to ninety days to get hold of your cash might dissuade you from buying that DVD box set or those simply must-have shoes. Yes, I know the heel is exactly the height you've been looking for, the colour matches 80% of your clothes and they'll make your legs look longer and your bum look smaller, but they're only going to sit at the bottom of your wardrobe with the other 150 pairs.

If you can be trusted with your money, however, some accounts will allow you a limited number of penalty-free withdrawals a year – perhaps two or three – as long as you keep a minimum amount of cash in your account. Some accounts will also offer you a yearly bonus if you do not make any withdrawals during the twelve months.

The key point to remember, however, is, if you are good with money and don't need a notice period to stop you spending, then don't bother unnecessarily tying up your money with one. If you can get the same level of interest or more on an instant-access account, go for one of those. You never know what's around the corner and having instant access to your money is always handy.

'Over the last few years the difference in rates between notice and no-notice accounts has narrowed,' adds Ms Thrussell at

Moneyfacts. 'In 2004 you would've received almost 0.35% more for tying your funds into a notice account compared with just 0.08% now. So the incentive to invest your savings within a notice account with rigid terms now seems a little pointless – the reward has virtually disappeared.'

Savings accounts: things to ponder

- Need to get hold of your money quickly? If so, stick to easy- or instant-access accounts.
- Don't mind managing your account online, by post or over the phone? Good, because that's often where you'll find the best interest rates.
- Not afraid to tie your money up in the long term? Then plump for a savings-bonds or term account. They pay some of the market's highest rates of interest, but remember that the rate they're offering is fixed.
- Worried about rising interest rates? If so stay clear of the fixed rates offered on regular savings or savings-bonds accounts and go for the variable rates offered on instant-access accounts. Their rates should go up in line with base rates.

Option 3: Regular savings accounts

At first glance regular savings accounts look amazing. At the time of writing, Barclays has just launched a regular savings account that paid interest of 12.5% – more than double the market's best-paying instant-access rate. The trouble with these deals is that they are riddled with catches and conditions.

With the Barclays deal, for example, you also have to open a current account with the bank, which pays interest of virtually 0%; you can only save a maximum of £250 a month; you can't make withdrawals without being penalised; and you can save only for a period of up to a year. After the one-year period is finished the money you have saved is then transferred into your low-paying Barclays current account.

The good thing about these accounts is that the rate is fixed as well as being very high. For those of you who already have a current account with Barclays, or whichever bank is peddling similar regular savings deals, and who can commit to saving regularly each month without needing access to the money, these deals can be very attractive options.

If it requires your moving your current account, which pays one of the market's highest rates of interest as well as one of the lowest overdraft rates, you need to think carefully about what you're giving up.

Is your money safe?

Pretty much. A high-street, online, telephone or postal bank account is a low-risk home for your money. Legitimate UK banks rarely go under and if they do you are protected by the Financial Services Compensation Scheme.

That safety net means you are guaranteed to get back your first £2,000 and 90% of the next £33,000 if your bank goes belly up (and, as you know, there's a lot of belly to go up). But there are no guarantees beyond that. If you ever reach the situation in which you have more than £35,000 in your account, you should look to save the remainder in another account to reduce your risk and take advantage of these guarantees.

Option 4: Term and bond accounts

In return for agreeing to tie your money up at a fixed rate of interest for a set period of time – anything from six months to five years – savings bonds or term accounts, as they are sometimes known, will usually offer you the market's highest rates of interest.

These accounts are geared towards people who want a guaranteed income with minimum risk and who are happy to lock away sizeable sums of their money for sizeable periods of time.

But remember: fixed rates are attractive only if you think interest rates are on their way down or if the rate you've signed up to is big enough to make base-rate increases less of an issue.

Don't forget that the Fat Belly banks are the experts when it comes to all things financial and, if they're offering fixed-rate accounts way above the best instant-access accounts, it probably means that they think interest rates are on their way up.

Which means the rate they are offering might look good now but in three years' time it might not look so good. Keep that in mind, because you may not be able to get to your money before the end of the three- or five-year period and, even if you can, you will be subjected to steep penalties for doing so.

The Jargonator: AER

AER – or the annual equivalent rate – not only takes into account the interest rate but how often it is paid. Normally, bank and building-society accounts pay interest annually and, when this happens, the AER will be the same as the gross (before-tax) rate of interest. If, however, the same interest rate is paid more frequently, such as monthly, the AER will be higher. For example, an interest rate of 4.65% paid monthly has an AER of 4.75%. If you are trying to find the best savings account, always make sure you compare like with like, i.e. a gross savings rate with another gross savings rate or an AER with another AER.

Gross and net interest rates

The **gross rate** of interest is the rate of interest before tax. If you are a non-taxpayer you can register to get your interest paid gross. To register for this all you need to do is fill out an R85 form, which is available at your chosen bank or building society as well as your local tax office. Without this declaration, your Fat Belly bank will automatically deduct a fifth (20%) of your interest or two-fifths (40%) if you are a higher-rate taxpayer.

The **net rate** of interest is the rate of interest after tax has been deducted. So, for a basic-rate taxpayer (20%) a gross rate of 5% is reduced to 4% after savings tax has been deducted. If you pay tax at 40% the same 5% rate becomes just 3%.

What are my other options?

Well, there are lots of other savings options at your disposal. But, because in this section we are looking only at low-risk homes for your money, we are not ready to touch on the likes of shares, corporate bonds and property or look at investing in stamps, art and wine just yet. But that doesn't mean your other options have to be boring.

For starters, what about putting as little as £100 or as much as £30,000 into a tax-free savings product that could net you a cash prize of £1 million a month. No, it's not quite the National Lottery – you can't lose the money you play with but you do put your interest on the line.

Premium Bonds: it could be you

More than a quarter of the money invested with National Savings & Investments (NS&I), the government outfit that raises money for public spending by providing a range of savings and investment products, is tucked away in Premium Bonds.

Set up in 1956, Premium Bonds are not strictly speaking a savings product, because, instead of getting a regular rate of interest on your money, you rather more imaginatively get a chance to win one of 1.34 million monthly tax-free prizes. Prizes are picked at random by NS&I's ERNIE (Electronic Random Number Indicator Equipment).

The size of the prize fund depends on interest rates (the higher interest rates are, the larger the prize fund will be) and at the time of writing the odds of winning a prize were 24,000 to 1. Basically, the more Premium Bonds you hold, the more chance you have of winning some cash. But don't get carried away. The chance of a £1 bond walking away with one of the two monthly £1 million prizes is 16 billion to 1.

Anyone over the age of sixteen can buy Premium Bonds but parents, grandparents and guardians can also buy them for kids under that age. The minimum you can buy is £100 worth, which will get you 100 bonds that have an equal chance of winning a cash prize. The maximum you can buy is £30,000 worth.

Prizes range from £50 to £1 million and the number of prizes depends on how many bonds are eligible to take part each month. At the time of writing there were almost 1,155,000 £50 prizes, 273,104 £100 prizes, a little over 7,000 £500 prizes, 2,346 £1,000 prizes, 194 prizes of £5,000, 97 of £10,000, 38 of £25,000, 19 of £50,000, 10 of £100,000 and 2 £1 million prizes.

You are able to win prizes only once your bonds have been held for one complete calendar month and, rather than just cashing in your winnings, you can instead opt to have them automatically buy you more bonds.

If you win one of the two monthly £1 million jackpots, NS&I contacts you in person. Otherwise, you will receive notification by post. This is sent to the last address that NS&I has for you – so let them know if you move. There is currently over £30 million in unclaimed prizes. You can check whether you have an unclaimed prize by punching your holder's number into the Premium Bond prize checker on NS&I's website (www.nsandi.com) or by contacting the Premium Bond department on 0845 964 5000.

'Premium Bond sales have soared in recent years with the amount invested in the last five years more than the previous 45 years put together,' NS&I told me. 'People like the fact that their Premium Bond stake is a refundable investment, that their money is 100% secure, that they have a chance to win one of over a million prizes each month and that all prizes are tax-free.'

Premium Bonds: in numbers

- Twenty-three million people (almost 40% of the population) hold Premium Bonds.
- More than 32 billion eligible Premium Bonds go into each monthly draw.
- All Premium Bond prizes are free of UK income tax and capital-gains tax.
- Since the first Premium Bond prize draw in 1957, more than 140 million tax-free prizes worth £9 billion have been given away.
- The odds of each £1 unit winning a prize are fixed – currently at 24,000:1.
- Every eligible bond has a separate and equal chance of winning a prize, irrespective or when or where it was bought.
- There are currently more than 450,000 unclaimed Premium Bond prizes worth over £30 million.
- There is no time limit to claim a prize.
- The largest unclaimed prize is for £25,000. It is believed the winner emigrated to Canada, but efforts to trace them have failed.
- The monthly maximum prize – now £1 million – is a thousand times higher than it was in 1957.
- With average luck, an investor with £30,000 in Premium Bonds could win fifteen tax-free prizes a year – more than one a month.

But are they worth it?

Statistically speaking, no, but, if you like a flutter, yes. Premium Bonds are a fun way to save your money but, if you haven't already used your £3,000 tax-free cash ISA allowance, you are better off doing that first. Yes, I *know* you won't walk away with a million quid if you invest in a cash ISA but don't forget that the chance of a £1 bond winning the £1 million jackpot is 16 billion to 1 – slimmer than a supermodel on a sponsored famine.

Yes, there are 1.34 million prizes given away each month but just eight of these are £100,000 and only 15 are £50,000 with the overwhelming majority (1,155,000) set at just £50.

Tuck £3,600 (your full yearly allowance) into a cash ISA and you'll get back £229 worth of interest after the first year at a rate of 6% and £474 after two years. Put the same £3,600 into Premium Bonds and, although your chance of winning a prize is increased to 8 to 1, meaning you could win three cash prizes in two years, 99.4% of those prizes are either fifty or a hundred quid.

In fact, NS&I calculates that, on average, you'll earn a tax-free return of 3.15% from your Premium Bonds, which means that, if you held £3,600 worth of bonds, you would pull in £117 a year or a little over £237 after two years if you bought £3,600 worth of bonds and reinvested your winnings.

But, if you've already squeezed your cash ISA allowance dry and you like a flutter, then Premium Bonds may be a good option for you. At least your money is 100% secure, your winnings are tax-free and it can be fun imagining what you'd do with a million quid.

Five Premium Bond myths debunked
Myth 1: ERNIE is not random

The Government Actuary's Department (GAD) certifies the randomness of ERNIE and the Premium Bond draw. Each month, the results of the draw are sent to GAD, which carries out a number of statistical tests. Once it is satisfied the results of the draw are random, it issues NS&I with a certificate to that effect. Without this, NS&I is not allowed to publish the numbers or issue prizes.

Myth 2: You have to have the maximum (£30,000) holding to win

In July 2004, the winner of the £1 million jackpot had just £17 in Premium Bonds bought in 1959, while nine of the last twelve jackpot winners held less than the £30,000 maximum. The more bonds held, the better, but that doesn't mean prizes are won exclusively by higher-value holdings

Myth 3: Only new bonds win prizes

Each £1 bond has an equal chance of winning regardless of when it was bought. Bonds purchased more recently may seem to win more often but that is because there are more new bonds than old ones. Since the £1 million jackpot prize was introduced in April 1994, more bonds have been sold than in the preceding years put together.

Myth 4: Old bonds are left out of the draw

Premium bond numbers are not programmed into or stored in ERNIE, so no numbers can be left out of the draw. ERNIE's sole function is to generate numbers randomly. These are then matched against the existing eligible bond numbers.

Myth 5: Only bonds from the southeast win prizes

It may appear that holders in the southeast win more prizes but it is simply because there are more Premium Bonds held in the southeast compared with the rest of the UK. Over the last eighteen months, the £1 million jackpot winners have been from East Riding of Yorkshire, Tyne and Wear, Worcestershire, Devon, Berkshire, Gloucestershire, Cumbria, Surrey, Hampshire, Lincolnshire, the London Borough of Newham and Bristol.

Casebook

Elisabeth Johnson, 48, from Gloucestershire

I had always known about Premium Bonds since I was a kid because I have an older brother and sister who were each given a £1 bond when the system was first launched in 1956. I guess there were a lot of kids around at that time who were bought and still have nothing more than a £1 bond.

I think I bought my first bonds when I was eighteen, about £20 worth, although it wasn't until I was in my thirties that I started saving any serious amounts of money in Premium Bonds.

The main reason was that I was self-employed, which meant I had to pay my tax bill in one go at the end of the tax year rather than in monthly instalments, and so I used Premium Bonds as a place to store up the money I was going to use to pay my tax bill.

Because I was a higher-rate taxpayer, it seemed like a good idea, since not only was it safe and free from tax but there was always that chance I would win a big cash prize. Putting the money in a savings account seemed pointless given that I would have to pay 40% tax on the interest.

I tended to save the maximum amount during that period, which was then £20,000, and although I never won any of the big prizes I often won £50 and once I got a cheque through the post for £1,000.

I am a housewife now with a young son and so I don't ever have as much in Premium Bonds as I used to, but I've still got £6,000 worth, £3,000 of which is mine and £3,000 of which is in my son's name.

I know it might be a better idea for me to put that money in a cash ISA, where I would be guaranteed a fixed level of tax-free monthly interest, but I reckon I win a £50 prize at least once every other month so I'm happy with that.

National Savings Certificates

Thought a certificate was something you got as a kid when you jumped into a swimming pool with your pyjamas on to 'save' a rubber brick. Well, you'd be wrong. It turns out you can also buy them from your local post office with between £100 and £15,000 of your cash.

National Savings Certificates, first launched in 1916 as War Savings Certificates, offer a secure, tax-free home for your money. You can invest anything from £100 up to £15,000 in savings certificates without affecting your other tax-free options, such as ISAs. But be warned: unless you tie up your money for the full term, which could be as much as five years, you'll get back less interest than you'd hoped.

There are two main types: inflation-linked and fixed-interest certificates.

Inflation-linked savings certificates

If you are worried about inflation eating into your savings then you should have a long hard look at inflation-linked savings certificates – but only if you're willing to commit your cash for either three or five years.

Inflation-linked certificates guarantee that the money you've saved always beats inflation, as measured by the Retail Price Index. It does this by paying you the annual rate of inflation as well as a fixed rate of interest on top. And so, for example, the latest three-year inflation-linked certificate on offer, confusingly called the 14th Issue, pays 1.15% on top of the current level of the Retail Price Index.

This produces a gross rate in excess of 5%. Clearly not as much as some of the highest-paying Fat Belly bank accounts but it's tax-free and that means you'd have to find yourself an equivalent gross rate of more than 6% as a basic-rate taxpayer and more than 8% as a higher-rate taxpayer.

But in order to get the full interest rate on your savings you need to make sure you can tie up your money for the complete stretch. If you withdraw your cash before the three- or five-year period ends, you'll lose out. In fact, pull your money out during the first year and you won't earn any interest at all. After that you'll earn interest for each complete month you hold them. But be careful: the certificates are structured in a way that means the interest you get grows larger each year, so it pays to stay committed.

Fixed-interest certificates

If you want a guaranteed return on your money, then another option might be fixed-interest savings certificates. You won't earn the market's very top rates but you will know exactly how much interest you'll get each year.

The interest rates are fixed for the length of your chosen savings period, either two or five years, and, as with inflation-linked savings certificates, all of the interest you earn is tax-free – a particular draw for higher-rate taxpayers.

Again, you can invest anything from £100 up to £15,000 without affecting your other tax-free investments. The certificates are sold in issues (see the Jargonator on p114), which are dependent on current interest rates. If your crystal ball tells you interest rates are on the way up, then it's best to stay well clear. You'll only end up tying yourself into a set rate of interest while rates elsewhere go up.

To get the full interest on your certificates, which is paid out to you only in one go at the end, you again need to be sure you can tie your money up for the full term. If you cash them in early, you will lose out. As with inflation-linked savings certificates, pull your money out during the first year and you won't get any interest at all. After that, you'll earn interest for each complete set of three months you hold them.

Remember, like their inflation-linked brothers, fixed-interest certificates are structured in a way that means the interest you get increases each year – so stay with them.

What happens at the end of each term?

Shortly before your savings certificate reaches the end of its investment term, NS&I will write to let you know your options. You can (a) continue your investment in the next identical issue, (b) reinvest in a fixed- or inflation-linked-interest savings certificate of a different term or (c) cash in your investment. If you do not do anything, your money will be automatically reinvested in the next series or issue of the same product.

Are savings certificates right for me?

Yes if …

- you want to be sure that your savings will beat inflation or you want returns at guaranteed interest rates;
- you want to make the most of your tax-free investment opportunities;
- you have £100 or more to invest;
- you can leave your money untouched for two, three or five years.

No if …

- you want a regular income from your money;
- you think you may need access to your money at any time;
- you are a non-taxpayer, or pay tax only at the lowest rate.

The Jargonator: Issue

Savings certificates are sold in issues, each of which has its own number. For example, the latest inflation-linked savings certificates on offer are called issue 35. Whenever the interest rates NS&I offers change, maybe as a response to the Bank of England's base rate increasing or decreasing, NS&I releases a new issue. Each time a new issue goes on sale you can invest

>>
up to another £15,000 tax-free. NS&I normally releases several
new issues a year, for all of the two-, three- and five-year terms.

Retail Price Index

The Retail Price Index (RPI) shows the changes in the cost
of living. It reflects the movement of prices in a range of
goods and services we regularly use over time, such as food,
heating, housing, household goods, bus fares and petrol. Items
considered most important to us, such as housing and food,
are given a higher weighting in the overall index, while items
such as tobacco are given a lower weighting. NS&I measures
inflation using the RPI, not the newer Consumer Prices Index
(CPI), which doesn't include house prices.

Child trust funds

Another tax-free way to save money is through a child trust fund
(CTF). Needless to say, you'll need to have popped one out to benefit
from a CTF but it is also important to know that these are a little
different from the other savings options we have looked at, since any
wonga you stick into a CTF belongs not to you but to your kid.

Money you save into a CTF is owned by the whippersnapper and
can only be withdrawn by them, not Mummy or Daddy, when they
reach the tender age of eighteen. If you adore your kids and one
of the very reasons you initially started saving was to pay for your
child's university education, for example, then a CTF might suit you
down to the ground.

But, if the thought of letting an eighteen-year-old loose on many
thousands of your hard-earned pounds (up to £30,000 if you save
your annual allowance of £1,200 at a rate of 5%) makes you feel
slightly nervous, then you might want to skip to the next section.

CTFs are great in theory but if you can't trust the child you're
funding forget it.

What's it all about?

Any child born on or after 1 September 2002 is eligible to have a CTF. The beautiful part is that the government will give you a £250 voucher to start your child's fund when it's born and will add another £250 to the fund when your child reaches the age of seven. Children from lower-income families get an additional £250 at both stages. There is also talk that the government will make a further payment at the age of eleven, but at the moment that's just talk.

You, your friends and your relatives are then free to add a further combined sum of £1,200 a year into your child's fund, all of which is tax-free.

Can I buy shoes with the vouchers?

No. The vouchers must not be used for anything other than opening a CTF, of which there are three different types: a simple cash savings account, a stakeholder equity account (allowing your child to invest in a number of funds with charges capped at 1.5%) and a non-stakeholder equity account.

Even though CTFs are a very simple savings tool, choosing the most suitable home for your voucher and any additional money you pay in is not easy. This is because there are more than seventy different providers and distributors, including banks, friendly societies and fund managers, competing for your attention. A full list of CTF providers can be found on the government's child trust fund website at www.childtrustfund.gov.uk.

The simplest and safest option is to deposit your voucher into a straightforward savings account. The investment performance of the fund will depend on the interest rate the account offers. Lots of different providers, including Halifax and Nationwide, offer cash CTFs and if you decide to take that route you simply follow exactly the same rules you would when opening any other type of savings account, i.e. shop around, find the best-paying account and be wise to any catches.

To help you, details of the best cash CTFs can be found on the Moneyfacts website at www.moneyfacts.co.uk.

Like a cash ISA, a cash CTF offers you a low-risk way to save your money. But you might be better off taking more risk with your CTF allowance. Why? Because tucking money away in a CTF is a very long-term commitment.

The beauty of a cash ISA is that, as well as being able to save money tax-free, you can also get to your dough quickly. The money you invest in a CTF, however, can't be accessed until your child turns eighteen, and so the instant-access benefits of a low-risk savings account are lost.

Over the very long term, stocks and shares have historically outperformed savings accounts and, as a CTF is undeniably a very long-term venture, you might be better off investing your CTF allowance in a stakeholder equity or a shares account.

If you are totally freaked out by the stock market and would prefer to keep your £250 voucher and any additional money in a cash CTF, that's fine. Choose the highest-paying cash CTF and lob your money in there. But don't hang around. If you don't do anything with your voucher during the first twelve months after you receive it, the government will automatically open a stakeholder account for you, though you can transfer out of this.

So what is a stakeholder account?

Stakeholder accounts invest in a fund made up of a variety of different company shares. As a share-based investment, this is more risky than a cash account because the returns are not guaranteed. But stakeholder CTFs can be life-styled, meaning that your money is switched into less risky investments, such as bonds and cash, when the child reaches thirteen. This is to protect your investment from any sudden downturns in the stock market as your child gets closer to the age when he or she can access the money.

The main feature of a stakeholder account is its low annual

management charges. Legally, these must be no more than 1.5% a year – the equivalent of £1.50 on every £100 invested. Once the account has been set up, the provider must also be prepared to accept minimum top-ups of £10 a time. At the time of writing, the majority of parents had invested their government vouchers in a stakeholder account.

And a shares account?

The shares option, as the name suggests, is also a share-based investment but, unlike those of the stakeholder account, its charges are not capped. These accounts are generally aimed at more experienced investors who are looking for a wide investment choice or people who are prepared to take more risk.

CTFs in a nutshell

- A long-term savings and investment account where your child (and no one else) can withdraw the money when they turn eighteen.
- Neither you nor your child will pay tax on income and gains in the account.
- £250 voucher to start each child's account topped up by a further £250 when the child reaches the age of seven.
- Children in families receiving Child Tax Credit, with a household income of less than £14,155, will receive an extra payment of £250.
- A maximum of £1,200 each year can be saved.
- Money cannot be taken out once it has been put in – when your child is 18 they will be able to decide how to use it.
- Children can start to make decisions about how the money is managed when they are sixteen.
- At any time you can move the account to a different provider or change the type of account.
- The funds do not affect any of your benefits or tax credits.

Friendly societies

If you have used up all your other tax-free options to save your cash you may want to consider – particularly if you are a higher-rate taxpayer – friendly societies. Friendly-society savings plans allow you to save up to £25 a month or £270 a year tax-free. To qualify for tax-free status, however, your investment must run for at least ten years. Friendly-society plans are limited to one per person.

These types of savings are worthwhile only if you are prepared to tie your money up for the ten years. If you take your money out early you'll get clobbered with charges and the plan will lose its tax-free status. A further problem with these plans is that many of the societies that offer them deduct their fees during the first few years, known as frontloading, so, if you withdraw your money after only a couple of years, you might be left with a lot less than you put in. Not so friendly.

Friendly-society savings plans are a lot riskier than investing in a Premium Bond or a cash ISA, so proceed with caution and consider your other low-risk tax-free options first.

What is a friendly society?

A friendly society, sometimes referred to as a mutual society, is a financial organisation owned by its members and not shareholders. They have been around for yonks and historically people invested in these societies to protect themselves and their families from hardship in the absence of the welfare state.

These days, there is very little difference between a friendly society and a building society, but historically friendly societies were set up to provide insurance-style services, while building societies were set up to help their members buy houses. Friendly societies offer a variety of services including savings accounts, child trust funds, loans, credit cards as well as insurance.

PART 3:
INVEST
IT

Are you getting risky with me?

Right, if you've got this far in the book or if you've skipped straight to this section, it means you're interested in taking a little bit more risk with your cash.

If you're not happy about putting your money on the line, however – and by that I mean you're not interested in losing some or possibly all of the cash you invest – you should stick to keeping your money in very low-risk products, such as a high-street or Internet savings account, where you get back at least what you put in with some interest on top.

There's no shame in being cautious. There are some very good low-risk products on the market and, if you're a higher-rate taxpayer and you make use of your yearly £3,000 tax-free cash ISA allowance, for example, you can help yourself to returns equivalent to rates of around 8.5% before tax.

But, if you've squeezed your yearly cash ISA limit dry, paid off all your expensive outstanding debts and built up an emergency cash fund of at least three (or preferably six) times your monthly take-home pay, you're ready not just to save but also to invest the extra dough you have.

What *is* investing?

Investing, like its little savings brother, is about using your money to make more money. The difference is that you can make a lot more of it over the same period of time by investing your cash than you can by shoving it in a savings account.

In order to make that happen, however, you have to be prepared to take more risk with your money, which might mean losing some or all of it along the way.

Don't panic, though. Investing is not speculating. It's not about sticking your money on Damn That Horse Is Slow at the 3.30 at Kempton or buying a painting from a never-heard-of-before artist in the hope he or she makes it big and then snuffs it shortly afterwards.

While speculating is akin to splashing out on a few hundred lottery tickets, investing is about taking calculated risks – many of which will pay off and some of which won't – in order to give yourself more than a fighting chance of making some serious cash.

Crucial to this happening, however, is your need to learn to live apart from it. When you invest, you have to imagine you've sent your money off on a very long holiday with no forwarding address. Indeed, the longer you can live apart from your dosh the more risk you can afford to take with it and the more money you'll hopefully end up making.

If you have a pot of cash that you are waiting to use as a deposit on a house or flat you're buying next year, forget about putting that money at risk. Shove it in a top-paying savings account. But, if you can live without that same pot of cash for a number of years, it's actually reckless to be overly cautious with it.

Riskier investments, such as the stock market, can be a bit of a bumpy ride with short-term periods of very high rises as well as short-term periods of very steep falls.

But over the long term the stock market has tended to produce significantly higher rates of return than savings accounts. In fact, over the last fifty years you'd have received more than three times as much annual interest from the stock market as you would have from a Fat Belly bank's savings account.

Be warned, though. If you'd invested your money in the stock market in 1999 and taken it out in 2003, you would have got back less than half of what you'd put in. You can never outstay your welcome when it comes to investing in riskier assets. The longer you can hang around the better – that way you'll have enough time to recoup any losses if things go belly up.

What are my investment options?

Good question. There are three broad types of investment open to you: bonds, property and equities. There are also pooled investments, which lump your money together with that of other investors. If you've never heard these terms before, don't worry: we'll go through each one in more detail. The main thing to keep in mind is that, generally speaking, bonds are the least risky investment of the three and equities are the riskiest, leaving property to lay its foundations somewhere in the middle. Pooled investments, meanwhile, can be as risky or as conservative as you make them.

Bonds

Bonds are basically IOUs. In the way you'd lend money to your mate Clive for a few days you can also lend it to the government or a company for a set period of time, perhaps 5, 10 or 15 years.

Unlike Clive, however, the government or the company not only promises to pay you back your money at an agreed time but will also pay you a fixed amount of interest for every year or six months they have your dosh.

This income is known as the bond yield and it is generally higher than the interest you would get from a savings account, as there are more risks attached to putting your money in bonds, particularly ones issued by companies.

The biggest risk, of course, is that the company you lend your money to might not be around in twenty years' time when it comes to getting your dough back. But, to compensate for this, bonds issued by companies, which are called corporate bonds, pay out a much higher level of interest than bonds issued by the UK government, which are known as gilts.

It is almost 100% certain you'll get your money back if you invest in UK government bonds, making them very appealing to conservative investors, while corporate bonds appeal to those wanting to take more of a punt with their cash.

The Jargonator: Growth versus income

If you do not need to draw an income from your investments, whether it's equities, bonds or a managed fund, you are a **growth investor**. A growth investor is keener on reinvesting any interest or dividends in order to beef up their investments. An **income investor**, meanwhile, depends on their investments for an income, and tends to buy more low-risk investments.

Asset class

Bonds, equities, property and cash are all asset classes and the way you spread your money between asset classes is your asset allocation. A risky asset allocation consists mainly of shares and a conservative allocation consists of more bonds, property and cash.

Property

People seem to like investing in property, because it's something they immediately understand. Unlike the case with a bond or an equity, you can live, go to school or go to work in a property, and that makes it a very popular asset class for investors.

Making money from property means investing in things such as office blocks, shopping centres and even residential property, directly, via a fund or by owning shares in companies that hold and manage such properties.

Your return is generated by the rent that tenants pay and any increase in the value of the property. But if prices fall and/or expenses outweigh the rental income you could incur a loss.

The value of UK property may well have increased faster than Vanessa Feltz's waistline over the last few years, but remember that prices do fall and, when they plummeted in 1989 by more than a fifth, it took nine years for them to get back to where they were.

Also, remember that, as far as direct investment is concerned, property is awkward to buy and sell and you can't offload little bits here and there when you need the money. Unlike the case with cash, bonds or shares, you also need to spend money to maintain your property.

That said, property is an attractive asset class for investors because it provides a useful diversifier to shares. Since the stock market fell in 1999, for example, commercial property has risen at an average rate of about 10% a year.

Don't be blinded by past performance £

Don't choose an investment fund purely on the basis of how it has fared previously. A lot of research by men with beards has found that just because a fund has performed well in the past does not necessarily mean it will do so again.

Interestingly, however, those same bearded fellas found that funds that have performed badly in the past will probably continue to do so – so steer clear.

There are individual fund managers that have produced consistently good results and shoving your money into one of their funds is a very popular strategy. The problem is that the best managers are often poached by rival investment companies and it can be expensive moving your money from fund to fund to stay with them.

Equities

When you own shares – or equities, as they are also known – you own a little bit of the company you've invested in. The more equities you own, the bigger that stake is; the better that company performs, the more steak you'll be able to buy. If you're a veggie you can obviously swap that steak for an avocado or something, but it doesn't work quite so well as a joke.

Shares don't have a fixed price and how much you pay for them is based on people's general confidence in that particular company. So, for example, if everyone thinks Fat Belly Co. is going to do well in the future and turn in a large profit, everyone piles into Fat Belly Co.'s equities, forcing its share price to shoot up.

In numbers, if you paid £3 for a share and the price of that share jumped up by 50% to £4.50, perhaps because Fat Belly Co. announced record-breaking profits, you would be in a position to sell at a significant profit – especially if you owned a large number of shares.

The flipside of this, however, is that, if a company reports lower-than-expected profits or is affected by some negative publicity, people may lose confidence in that firm and decide to sell. This will negatively affect the price of your £3 share and, if you came to sell, it would be worth less than what you paid for it. Over a longer period, however, the company might be able to turn its fortunes around, increase the amount of money it makes and improve its profit margin – pushing the share price back up.

The other way to make money from shares is through dividends, which are a slice of the company's profits paid out to each shareholder, usually every six months. If a company is doing well and wants to reward its shareholders it may announce a big dividend, but if times are hard it may give you a big fat zero.

Pooled investments

Pooled investments, also known as packaged or collective funds, are where you pool your money together with that of other investors and stick it in a fund, managed by an investment professional. These include investment trusts, unit trusts and OEICs (open-ended investment companies, not the sound a pig makes), life-insurance policies and pension funds.

There are two big advantages to pooled funds: first, you can buy into a fund with just a few hundred pounds or maybe even as little as a tenner if you invest regularly; and, second, you don't have to make the decisions as to how your money is invested. You leave that to the manager of the particular fund you've stuck your money in.

Pooled funds manage hundreds of millions and sometimes billions of pounds of people's money and use it to buy a basket of investments. Only an individual with a really large sum of money could ever hope to diversify his or her portfolio in the same way.

So, if you want to invest in things such as shares, bonds and property, it makes sense for most of you to do so via a pooled fund, of which unit trusts and OEICs are probably the simplest. If you have a very large amount of money to invest with the expertise to match, however, you might want to do so directly.

With unit trusts and OEICs you can usually cash in part or all of what you have invested at any point, although some funds will hit you for an exit fee. You may also get regular dividends, which will vary in size. If you don't need this income you can have it automatically reinvested or, if an income is something you're particularly after, you can choose a fund that is designed to pay out higher levels.

For conservative investors who are looking for an income from their investments, bond funds, which chuck your money into a mixture of gilts, UK corporate bonds and overseas company bonds, are a good option. Cautious investors who are seeking growth from their money, meanwhile, might look at a balanced fund, which invests in a mixture of property, shares, cash and bonds.

Those wanting to take more risk should look at global growth funds, which not only invest predominantly in shares but also in companies from around the world. Remember, though, that these types of fund are very long-term investments and you should be prepared to wave goodbye to your money for at least five to ten years and preferably more if you can.

Yeah, but what kind of pooled fund do I need?

If you don't want to take any risk at all, keep your dough in a savings account. If you want to invest for one to three years and you want an income from your investments, consider a bond fund. For those happy to take more risk and be apart from their cash for at least three years, a balanced fund might be the best option, and if you can invest for at least five years you should take a look at equity funds.

What do I do with all these investments?

Whether you are a very experienced investor or a total novice, the most important thing is not to put all your eggs in one basket – otherwise they'll end up on your face.

If you have only a small amount of money to invest, it's probably best to do so via a pooled fund, where you have access to the skills of an investment professional and an already diversified portfolio.

If you have enough money to buy your investments directly, you need to make sure you create a portfolio that includes different asset classes and different business sectors, such as energy companies or banking firms, within each asset class. If you buy shares and bonds in thirty different companies you'll lose only a small amount of your total investment if one of those firms goes belly up.

Put your money in just one company and you run the risk of losing everything you've invested if the fan is hit by that brown stuff that stinks.

Deciding how to diversify your portfolio is known as asset allocation, and one of the easiest and most popular ways of doing that is to adopt the age-adjusted mix.

Quite simply that means taking your age, subtracting that from 100, putting a percentage sign at the end and then shoving that much of your total portfolio into shares. So if you're 35 years old, 65% of your dough should be tucked away in equities with the rest invested in a mixture of bonds, property and cash. And if you're 45? Then 55% should be invested in shares with the rest split among bonds, property and cash.

The idea behind this is to grow your cash and take more risk with your money when you're younger and to protect it and take less risk with it as you get older.

Five investing tips

1. **Pay the smallest amount possible in taxes. Consult a qualified expert to help you pay less tax. Often, the cost of advice is more than offset by the savings.**

2. **Don't invest your money in things you don't understand. Take the time to learn about an investment before you jump in.**

3. **Don't procrastinate about your investment choices. If you know you need to do something with your money, be proactive. Time can be your friend, but, if you wait too long, it can also be your enemy.**

4. **Be aware of investment fees and reduce them whenever possible. A small decrease in fees could add several thousand pounds to your savings.**

5. Ignore investment hype. There is a ceiling to how high any investment can go and eventually the bubble will burst and values will fall. It is often better to wait until the hype passes and then buy when the price has dipped.

The expert view: Managing your risk

Mark Dampier, head of research at Hargreaves Lansdown

There is a natural trade-off: big profits mean taking risks, while if you want security your returns will often be modest. The most basic way to manage risk is not to put all your eggs in one basket.

You might start by dividing your money into four pots: cash, bonds, property and shares. The idea is that the assets shouldn't all move in the same direction at once, so a sudden fluctuation in your portfolio's value becomes less likely.

Cash should be your instant-access fund for paying bills and in case of emergencies – aim for around six months' salary. Cash is low risk and secure, so you should also expect returns to be low. It also allows you the flexibility to take advantage of investment opportunities as they arise.

Bonds let you fix your level of income in advance. Unlike with cash, the value of your capital can fluctuate, so there's some risk involved. They will provide little growth, so will appeal less to younger investors.

Clearly not many people can afford to buy an entire **property**, but it is possible to buy commercial property funds as well as real-estate investment trusts, also known as REITs. Take care in this area, since you probably already have a huge property investment – your house!

Shares are probably the least understood asset class, but their risk means they can provide better returns over the long term. Companies seek to increase their profits each year, so over time the share prices of good companies should rise. Fortunately, it is easy to buy a unit trust or investment trust where a professional manager chooses the shares for you.

You should plan to hold riskier investments for at least ten years, so, if you'll need access to the money sooner, consider safer investments such as cash. Age is a crucial factor. If you're close to retirement, focus on generating an income while preserving existing capital.

It's often a bad sign when an investment becomes very popular, since you risk buying just when things begin to go wrong. Do your homework. Diversifying will help you manage risk only when you're buying into areas that represent good value for money. You don't have to use every asset class, but the majority of people find at least two and possibly three that are suitable for their needs.

First things first: get a pension

So, let's get this straight. You're looking to take more risk with your dough in the hope it'll grow into something big, or at least something bigger than it would in a high-interest savings account. Is that right?

And to get that something big you've probably already thought about investing your money in equities, bonds and property. Am I right? Well if I am – and you haven't told me I'm not yet – you should really think long and hard about investing that money in a pension.

You what?

OK, OK, let's not do anything hasty. I know pensions sound deathly boring and that you were hoping this section on investing was going to be a little sexier than the other sections we've looked at – but it makes sense.

Let's look at this rationally. We've already agreed that investing is a long-term venture but what could be more long term than a pension plan. Second, there's a strong chance that the reason you decided to invest your money in the first place is that it'll grow into a nice pot of cash you can use when you retire. Am I correct?

We'll assume I am, and that means that, by not investing the money you've earmarked for your retirement via a pensions vehicle of some sort and doing it another way, you are losing out on some very important tax breaks as well as missing out on the possibility that your employer will give you some 'free' money to play with.

OK, you've got my attention

Good. Let me make this clear: investing your dough in a pension scheme is the most tax-efficient long-term investment you can make. Why? Because your payments get topped up by the government.

The tax relief you get from the state should make contributing into a pension a no-brainer for basic-rate taxpayers and, especially, higher-rate taxpayers who have to pay tax at 40%.

In numbers, the reasoning is simple: a basic-rate taxpayer, who pays income tax at 22% (falling to 20% in April 2008), has to pay only £78 into a pension to get £100 worth of investment, be it in equities or bonds or whatever, while a higher-rate taxpayer has to cough up only £60 to get the same £100 worth of investment.

Not only that, but the money you invest in a pension plan grows free of any income or capital-gains tax and it's only when you draw (take out, nothing to do with pencils) an income from your pension at retirement that the government puts on its hoody and robs you of tax, by which time you may well have slipped into a lower tax bracket anyway.

And on top of these tax breaks you should also be able to take up to 25% of the money you've stuck into your pension as a tax-free lump sum. That's right, a tax-free lump sum to make that lump sum of yours even lumpier.

Pensions: a tax relief

If you want to invest for your retirement, do it via a pension fund. It's the most tax-efficient way to invest for your future. For example, if you want to put £10,000 into your pension the government will pay £2,200 of this if you are a basic-rate taxpayer, meaning it'll cost you just £7,800, while if you're a higher-rate taxpayer it'll only cost you £6,000. Even non-taxpayers, such as children or low earners, are entitled to tax

»

relief of 22% on contributions of up to £3,600.

And it doesn't stop there. Any money you invest in your pension plan will grow free of UK capital-gains tax and income tax, and when you come to retire 25% of what you've amassed can be withdrawn as a tax-free lump sum. Also – for those of you who like to plan these things – if you die before you start enjoying your pension the money can be passed on to your spouse, or anyone else you've nominated, free of inheritance tax. Not nice to think about but, at 40%, neither is inheritance tax.

What about that 'free' money you were talking about?

Ah, yes, the free money. Remember your first day at work when no one said hello to you and your cheeks hurt because of that permanent smile you were wearing. OK, well on that first day you were probably also given a load of information about the benefits your company offers.

If you were lucky, there may have been something about subsidised gym membership, possibly health insurance, an interest-free loan to pay your yearly travel costs and details about something called an occupational pension scheme.

Perhaps your eyes glazed over at that point, but the key thing to remember when it comes to occupational pension schemes is that, if your employer offers one, you need to join it.

Join now. Put the book down, run down the corridor to your HR manager's office, wink at the post -room boy along the way or, if you're feeling really charitable, that temp no one's ever bothered to speak to, and sign up. Your company will give you 'free' money.

As I've said already, if you want to invest for the future it would be foolish not to do so via a pension scheme because of the tax breaks you get. And, if that pension plan happens to be an *occupational* pension scheme, you've hit the jackpot and it's time to dish out the 'high fives'

– your employers are going to dip into their pockets as well.

That's right, your company will invest money too. In order to get that dough, however, it's likely you'll have to part with some of your own cash. But that's not a problem. We've already worked out that a pension scheme is the best long-term way to invest – and you were going to invest your money via some sort of pension scheme, anyhow.

Some firms will double what you put in up to certain limits; some will match what you put in up to maybe 3 or 5% of your salary; others will pay into your pension without your having to make any contributions at all – cannily named noncontributory pension schemes.

If you need any more convincing, look at it as a way of getting yourself a pay rise. Do you, like many, feel underpaid and overworked? Have you recently asked for a pay increase only to be told by your boss that his or her hands are tied and that you're top of the list of people to get one next year? Well, there's no need to wait a year. Sign up to your occupational pension scheme today and get a pay rise straight away.

It might mean you have to invest 5% of your monthly salary but that amount could be doubled. That means that if you earn £30,000 a year you'll effectively get yourself a pay increase of £3,000. And, if your employer only matches what you put in, that's still a pay rise of £1,500 a year. It's true you can't access that money until you retire, but isn't that exactly what you're investing for? An occupational pension scheme, like the free tea and biscuits your company may offer, is a perk of the job – just make sure you tuck into it as much as you do the bourbons.

A sobering thought

If there was ever an incentive to start investing in a work-related or private pension scheme, then the amount of money you'll get from the basic state pension has to be it. The full basic state pension is less than £85 a week for a single person and less than £135 a week for a married couple – no more than £67.50 a week each.

What's more, blokes must have paid at least 44 years of National Insurance contributions to get that £85 while women must have clocked up at least 39 years. The bad news is that the number of years required for women is also set to rise to 44 years with the female state pension age being increased from 60 to 65.

In the meantime, if you're a bloke and you've only clocked up 20 years of National Insurance contributions, which can seem like a lifetime in itself, you'll qualify for only £38.76 a week. For women that would be £43.81. And any fellas who have paid less than 10 years' National Insurance contributions can look forward to a big fat zero at retirement.

Women need to be extra careful. According to the Department of Work and Pensions, around 2 million women aren't building up any entitlement to a state pension at all while only 23% of them are on course to get their full allowance because they're either earning too little or have taken time off work to raise their children.

For those who have taken time out to bring up children, or care for relatives, you may qualify for the Home Responsibilities Protection Scheme, which effectively pays your National Insurance contributions for the years you're not working. Contact the Pension Service on 0845 606 0265 for details.

What if my tight-fisted employer pays nothing into the scheme?

Employers are not obliged to offer an occupational pension scheme and may instead offer something called a group personal pension scheme or a stakeholder pension scheme.

A group personal pension scheme, which is run by an insurance company, does not require your company to pay into it. Neither does a stakeholder pension scheme, which is like a personal pension but with some special features, such as a cap on charges and flexible contributions.

If your company has five or more employees and does not provide either an occupational pension scheme or a group personal pension scheme it must offer access to a stakeholder pension scheme. If yours doesn't, contact the Pensions Advisory Service on 0845 601 2923 for help.

But, just because your employer doesn't pay into these schemes, there's no need to write them off. It can still make sense to invest your money via a scheme your employer has set up rather than one you've organised yourself.

This is because the actual process of setting up, using and maintaining a pension scheme is not cheap. It's a complex business that requires input from a number of professionals, such as lawyers, actuaries and fund managers, and they all need to be paid. On top of that, you've got the costs incurred by buying and selling the bonds or equities you're investing in.

The higher the charges, the less money left for you when you come to retire. Investing via a workplace scheme cuts down on those costs. Your company may have negotiated favourable terms and that's all the better for you. Yes, it's not ideal that your employer is not contributing, but your money won't be so readily gobbled up by expensive charges and so it's still a good idea.

Something to cheer you up

The good news, however, is that from 2012 every worker aged 22 or over who earns at least £5,000 and not more than £33,500, who doesn't already contribute to a company pension, will be automatically enrolled into what's known as the National Pension Savings Scheme (NPSS).

The idea is that any tight-fisted employer not currently offering its staff a pension scheme into which it tops up workers' contributions will be forced to do so by 2012. You can opt out of the scheme if you wish but doing so means you'll miss out on that pot of 'free' company money.

Under the new rules workers will be able to pay 4% of their salary into a personal account and employers will have to add an extra 3%. The government, meanwhile, has also promised another 1% in the form of tax relief.

Despite the fact the NPSS is limited to those earning less than £33,500, it is estimated that it will give an additional 10 million people, who don't already benefit from a company contributed pension scheme, access to a plan that's topped up.

But the proposal has its critics. The most obvious flaw is that it does nothing for the self-employed. Another problem is that retirement income earned under the NPSS will reduce savers' entitlement to means-tested benefits. Put another way, people won't profit from every penny they invest because some of that money will disqualify them from receiving state benefits. In a few cases, some people might actually end up worse off.

Also, some campaigners are worried that companies currently offering more generous pension schemes may see the reforms as an opportunity to cut their costs and reduce their pension contributions down to the proposed NPSS 3% level.

According to figures from the National Association of Pension Funds, the professional body for occupational pensions, UK employers currently pay 16% of their workers' annual wages into salary-related occupational schemes – more than five times the proposed NPSS amount – while those running money-purchase schemes, which rely on stock market growth, pay in 6%.

In fact, a survey by Barclays Financial Planning of 200 small to medium-sized business employers found that 18% might close their current pension schemes in favour of the NPSS, while almost a third agree that the new proposals will result in a levelling down of company pension schemes.

A man in a suit at Barclays said, 'The scheme will have invaluable benefits in increasing employee contributions. However, as our research highlights, there is a strong danger that employees currently participating in their company pension scheme will see a decrease in the contributions made by their employer.'

But this is just guesswork. On the whole, the NPSS is very good news for those of you clocking in and out at a company that pays diddly squat into your pension. But don't wait until 2012 to start your investment drive. Even if you're investing without company contributions, the earlier you start the better.

Imagine that …

… you kicked your smoking habit and used the money you spent on cigarettes to bung into a pension. How much do you reckon you'd have by the time you retire at 65? I'll put you out of your misery: you'd have a whopping £265,000. In fact, if you increased the amount you put into your pension each year by 2%, which is roughly how much the price of a packet of fags goes up annually, you'd have a cool £353,000.

A man in a necktie at Virgin Money Pensions said, 'There are an estimated 1.48 million smokers aged between twenty and twenty-four in the UK. If they all gave up smoking at twenty and put the money into a private pension instead, their combined retirement funds when they reached sixty-five would amount to an astonishing £392 billion. And that's without increasing their contributions every time the government puts the price of cigarettes up.'

But it doesn't just have to be smoking you give up. It's amazing to think that saving the equivalent of 200 packs of fags a year (around £80 a month) could grow into more than a quarter of a million quid by the time you're 65.

What about walking or cycling to work each day instead of taking the train, bus or Tube? Or how about taking in a packed lunch rather than buying it from some overpriced sandwich shop with a funny name, which somehow reckons two slices of bread, a little bit of butter, cheese and a trace of sweet pickle can cost up to three quid?

One of the biggest reasons people don't pay into their pension is that they think they can't afford it. But it doesn't take much to build yourself up a tidy sum of money, and there are many things you can cut down on or stop to free up a little bit of cash.

That man in a necktie at Virgin Money Pensions, who has a bee in his bonnet about smoking, added, 'If young smokers knew that their lifetime habit could cost them a third of a million pounds in lost pension, they might think twice about lighting up again. Comparing the cost of smoking with the cost of your pension demonstrates how over time relatively small amounts invested regularly can grow into a substantial pension fund.'

Non-work-related schemes

If you're self-employed, belong to a very small company that doesn't offer a workplace scheme or want to invest outside of your workplace scheme, you're going to have to set up a pension plan yourself.

The costs to you will be higher but remember: you still get all the same tax breaks you would via a workplace scheme and the beauty of some personal pensions, such as self-invested personal pensions (SIPPs), is that you get a lot more say over how your money is invested.

In fact, a SIPP not only allows you to invest directly in shares or bonds but also allows you to stick your money in gold bullion, hotels, children's homes, student halls of residence, prisons, hospitals and hospices and residential property via a managed fund. A personal pension, including a stakeholder pension, is open to anyone whether or not you are employed, self-employed or unemployed but you must be aged between 18 and 75. There is no upper limit to the total amount of money you can build up, although there are limits on the amount of tax relief you will get.

A personal pension scheme will give you one or more of the following benefits:

- **a pension during retirement, which can start at any age between 50 (rising to 55 by 2010) and 75;**
- **a tax-free lump sum at retirement of up to 25%;**
- **a pension payable to your widow, widower, civil partner or other dependant(s);**
- **a tax-free lump sum, payable if you die before retirement to your widow, widower, civil partner or other dependant(s).**

A stakeholder pension is a low-cost version of a private pension, which has to meet certain standards and conditions. For example, the pension provider cannot charge you more than 1% of the money you've built up in your fund as an administration charge.

For some people, a stakeholder pension may be the best option, since they offer greater flexibility than other personal pensions because you can stop paying into them without having to pay a penalty, and restart whenever you wish. You may also be able to vary the timing and the amount of money you whack in.

The Jargonator: Occupational pension scheme

An occupational pension scheme is a pension plan set up by your employer that allows you to save money for your retirement. They are hard to beat as a way to save for your future, since your company pays into the scheme as well. A salary-related scheme, also known as a defined-benefit scheme, promises you a certain level of pension in relation to how much you earn, while a money-purchase scheme provides you with a pension dependent on how much you pay in and how well your investments do. If your investments suck, the amount you get back sucks. With a salary-related scheme you almost always have no say in how your money is invested, but with most money-purchase schemes you are able to make broad investment choices.

Annuity

Before A-Day you had to buy an annuity to get hold of the cash you had invested in your pension fund. Those were the rules. You were allowed to take up to 25% as a tax-free lump sum, but the rest you basically had to give to an insurance firm in return for an annual income. The problem with most annuities is that they run out exactly when you do. So, if you pop your clogs twenty weeks into your retirement instead of twenty years, that's all you get and nothing is passed on to your family.

Under new rules, however, you also have the option to draw an annual income from your pension pot while the rest of your fund remains invested. If you keel over early the remainder of your cash can be used to provide a dependant's pension.

But it all seems a bit complicated

True. Pensions, whether organised through your work or by yourself, have had an annoying habit of being overly complex. But, in an effort to simplify the pensions landscape and encourage more people like you to invest via a pension, the government overhauled the system on 6 April 2006, known as A-Day in the pension world.

In a nutshell, eight main sets of pensions rules were replaced with one, designed to make the whole thing easier to understand. The main changes included the following.

Pension schemes: You can now have as many pension schemes as you want. So, for example, if you're a member of a company pension you can also now open one, two, three or more private pensions.

Pension contributions: There is now a simple annual allowance for pension contributions. Each tax year you can pay in the equivalent of 100% of your annual salary and qualify for tax relief. This is subject to a cap, which started life as £215,000 but will grow by £10,000 a year until it reaches £255,000 in 2010–11. If your savings increase by more than this you'll have to pay tax of 40% on the excess. Low and non-earners can contribute up to £3,600 and qualify for tax relief.

Big pension pots: There is a new limit, called the lifetime allowance, to how much you can hold in your one, two, three or more pension funds before it gets whacked for tax at 55% on the excess. The limit was set at £1.6 million and will rise by £50,000 a year until it reaches £1.8 million in 2010–11.

And small pension pots: If your total pension pot is worth less than £15,000 you will have the opportunity to take the whole lot as a cash lump sum (some of which will be liable for tax) rather than turning it into a tiny annual pension salary.

Tax-free lump sums: The new tax rules will allow virtually all pension schemes to let you take up to 25% of your investments in the form of a tax-free lump sum.

Pension income: Before A-Day you had to convert your pension savings into an annuity by the time you were 75 but now you don't. You must still start drawing your pension by the time you are 75 but you don't have to use an annuity to do so.

Death benefits: It is now possible to provide a death benefit up to your lifetime allowance, which will be £255,000 by 2010–11. Previously, under the old rule, you were offered four times your salary as a death-in-service benefit.

Retirement age: The age at which you can draw your private pension will increase from 50 to 55 for both men and women by 2010. But A-Day introduced flexible retirement, allowing people in occupational pension schemes to continue working while drawing their pension, where the scheme rules allow it.

Pensions versus ISAs

A number of pension scandals, such as Robert Maxwell's theft of £450 million from the Mirror Group's pension scheme or the more than a million workers wrongly persuaded to leave good company pension schemes in favour of inferior personal ones during the late eighties and early nineties, have made a lot of people anxious about pensions.

As a result many individuals are now using their £7,000-a-year (rising to £7,200 in April 2008) tax-free ISA allowance as a way to save for their retirement instead of bunging their money into a pension plan. But is this a good idea?

In short, no. The big difference between a pension and an

ISA is when you get your tax benefit. With a pension, you make contributions out of your pre-tax earnings but get taxed on the income when you draw your pension. With an ISA, you contribute out of your post-tax earnings but get tax benefits when you cash your investments in.

What gives pensions the edge, however, is that you can take up to 25% of the proceeds as a tax-free lump sum, which means you get tax relief not just on the way in but also on the way out.

Also, most people's retirement income is lower than their salaries, which may mean they are taxed at a lower rate. For example, someone currently earning around £40,000 a year could get 40% tax relief on their pension contributions but pay only basic-rate tax of 22% (falling to 20% in April 2008) once they've retired.

What's more, if you invest via an ISA and you lose your job, you'd have to use up most of what you'd saved before you qualified for any state benefits. With a pension that's not the case. Any dosh you invest via a pension is also protected if you are declared bankrupt.

Yes, ISAs are a much more flexible way to invest your dough because you don't have to wait until you're 50 or 55 to get your sweaty palms on it. But being able to get hold of your money easily may mean there's nothing left for you when you retire.

The expert view: How much should you put into your pension?

Justin Modray, independent adviser at Bestinvest

Putting money away for your retirement is very much like exercise: you know you should, but there's always something more enjoyable to do instead.

But the simplest way to do it is via a pension and, whether it's through your employer or a personal plan, both have the added benefit of tax handouts. In most instances you can also take up to a quarter of your fund as a tax-free lump sum when you retire.

Of course, there's no such thing as a free lunch. You cannot touch your pension monies until at least age 50 (rising to 55 from 2010) and, when you eventually receive an income from your pension, it's taxable. Nonetheless, pensions are a sensible option for most people.

But how much should you contribute? Let's start with the bad news. Saving towards retirement is becoming increasingly expensive because we're all generally living longer. If you retire at 60 with a life expectancy of 85, then buying an income will cost more than if you had a life expectancy of 75, because pension providers have to pay out for longer. The good news is that saving sooner rather than later can make a significant difference to your pension at retirement.

Using modest assumptions about future investment returns and salary increases, you need to save around 12% of your salary from age 25 to enjoy a pension of about half your salary at retirement at 65. This rises to 18% if starting at age 35 and 30% if starting at age 45. Always remember that there is no time like the present when it comes to pensions.

If your employer offers a scheme, joining is definitely a good idea. This is because your employer will often contribute on your behalf and, in the case of final-salary pensions, shoulder the investment risk. In recent years companies have learned to their cost that investment risk can be high, subsequently pumping millions of pounds into their final-salary schemes to cover shortfalls. Unsurprisingly, most now shy away from these schemes and instead offer employees money-purchase pensions.

Money-purchase occupational pensions and personal pensions are very similar. You invest your money in a range of investment funds while you are working and convert the pension fund to an income when you retire. Of course, the amount of pension income you eventually receive largely depends on the size of your pension fund at that time, which in turn depends on how much you contribute and the performance of your investments.

And that varies widely depending on the quality of the fund manager and how much risk they take. Stock market funds generally perform much better than cash over time, but can give you sleepless nights when markets fall. This means that, while they make sense 10–30 years before retirement, you should gradually move towards safer funds, such as bond funds, as you approach the big day.

You don't need braces to buy and sell shares

And nor do you need a pinstripe suit, cufflinks, shiny shoes or slicked-back hair. Anyone – and that includes you with your skirt tucked into your knickers and you with your jumper on inside out – can invest in shares.

It's true you'll have to get your head around a bit of jargon and it's fair to say you'll have to get used to taking a bit of risk with your cash, but shoving money into shares (also known as equities) is not restricted to blokes who look like that plonker from the film *Wall Street* – you know, the one played by Michael Douglas, Gordon Gekko or something.

You too can make money from equities. You're big enough, ugly enough and certainly clever enough to put your money successfully into shares, whether it's through a pooled fund or by investing directly – you just need to get a few ground rules straight first.

OK but what's so special about shares?

Well, a host of different studies from different organisations on different investments in different countries have come to one conclusion: shares have been by far the best-performing asset over time.

According to figures from investment bank Barclays Capital, £100 invested in equities in 1945 would be worth more than £4,000 now if all the dividends had been reinvested. The same amount shoved into government bonds would be worth just £164.

What's more, another study from investment bank CSFB shows that UK equities have produced annual returns of 7.3% since 1918 compared with returns of 2.3% for bonds and just 1.6% for cash.

That might not sound like much, but the beauty of compound interest means that £10,000 invested over twenty years in shares would put almost £41,000 in your pocket compared with around £16,000 from bonds and £14,000 from a Fat Belly bank account.

But that doesn't mean you shouldn't be careful. Had you invested that same £10,000 in 1999 and taken the money out in 2003 you would've been left with £5,000 less than what you started with.

Don't be a div head with your dividends

Figures from the investment bank Barclays Capital show that £100 invested in 1899 would now be worth close to £23,000 in real terms if all the dividends had been reinvested. Guess how much you would have got back if you didn't reinvest. Go on, guess. Fifteen thousand? No. Ten thousand? No. Five thousand? Not even close. If you had saved not one penny of the dividends your shares had paid out since 1899, that hundred quid of yours would be worth just £200 in real terms.

So what's the lesson we can learn from this? Simple, really: reinvest your dividends. If you are investing for your retirement or for something far off in the future and you don't need to rely on an income from what you've put away, please, for the love of God, plough those dividends back in. You'll be the envy of all your mates at bingo.

So how do I stop that happening to me?

By sticking around. You can never eliminate all the risks attached to investing in equities, but you can reduce them, and the best and easiest way of doing that is to keep your money tied up for the long haul.

If you look at a graph showing the performance of the FTSE 100 (see the Jargonator on p155) over a short period, such as three months, it looks like an angry mountain range with very steep peaks and deep troughs. These troughs and peaks are known as volatility, and the bigger the distance between the peaks and troughs, the bigger the volatility.

Look at the same graph over five years, however, and the mountain range looks a lot less angry – happy, almost – and there's a definite sense of its sloping upwards. From one day to the next, the prices of the shares you've bought will jump around more than a kangaroo on a trampoline but, over time, history tells us they'll go up.

You have to become less bothered by short-term fluctuations. The worst thing you can do is invest in a basket of shares or a pooled fund and then pull your money out at the first moment your investments slide. Not only will you have lost money by the fact your shares are worth less but you'll have also had to fork out on unnecessary trading costs.

But what if I panic?

Don't. The market is volatile – accept it. If the price of your shares drops there is no need to get rid of them unless something fundamental has changed about the company you're investing in.

It's very tempting to throw in the towel when the brown stuff hits the fan. But the truth is, when the price of the shares you are holding slides, that is likely to be the precise time you should be buying more. When everybody is selling it could be that you should be buying.

From an emotional point of view that can be hard to do, but, rationally speaking, it's a sensible option. Averaging down, to give it its posh name, is the process of buying more shares in a company as it falls in value so that the size of your overall portfolio stays the same.

For example if you buy 1,000 shares at a price of £2, costing you £2,000, and the price of your shares falls to £1, leaving you with £1,000 worth of stock, you should think about buying another 1,000 shares to bring your total holdings back up to £2,000. That means if the shares you've bought recover and the price bounces back up to £2 you would have made a healthy profit of £1,000.

But never, ever average down if the fundamentals of the company you've invested in have changed for the worse – you'll simply be sending good money after bad. In the words of Warren Buffet, the billionaire investment guru, 'Should you find yourself in a chronically leaking boat, energy devoted to changing vessels is likely to be more productive than energy devoted to patching leaks.'

Going green: ethical investing

£

If your principles matter more to you than your profits, you might want to consider investing your cash ethically. Ethical investing is all to do with being more selective about the companies you shove your money into and picking shares in companies that are not (a) causing damage to the environment, (b) exploiting their workers by paying low wages, (c) using child labour and (d) producing products that are considered harmful or dangerous, such as cigarettes and pornography.

It's important to remember that basing your investment decisions on ethical principles may not provide you with the greatest returns, but the theory is that companies making a positive contribution run less risk of getting into trouble with regulators, are less involved with costly court actions, are less likely to have people boycotting their products or have workers going on strike – all of which can have a negative effect on their share prices.

The best and most popular way to invest ethically is via a managed fund, since it can be difficult to judge on your own whether or not a particular company is operating ethically. These managed funds work in the same way as other conventional funds, in that the fund manager buys baskets of

"

shares in a particular sector, but before a decision is made as to which shares are chosen the manager also weighs up two sets of criteria – one positive and one negative.

Negative screening is when a fund manager actively weeds out the companies that are involved in businesses such as tobacco, deforestation, the arms trade, pornography and animal testing, and omits them from the group of funds he will invest in, while positive screening involves choosing companies with a strong antipollution record, for example.

There are more than fifty funds available that you can invest in but, as with anything, check what the costs are as well as their performance over at least the past three years. Also, make sure you choose a fund that suits your principles the best. If you care more about not investing in arms companies than you do gambling firms, make sure you pick a fund that does that.

The websites www.eiris.org and www.ethicalinvestors.com are good places to start your search.

OK, but what do you mean by fundamentals?

Let's imagine you've already done some homework, read a few newspapers and decided that the biggest thing to affect the economy over the long term is the fact that everyone is living longer. Fifteen years ago people used to snuff it at an average age of 73.8, but now we pop our clogs at an average age of 79.

Knowing that, you've decided you want to invest your cash in the pharmaceuticals sector (old people love painkillers) and after examining a few companies in that area you've chosen one you like.

That means you've looked at its company reports, worked out whether or not it is well managed, what its plans are for the future, who its competitors are, if its profits and turnover have been growing steadily over the last few years, whether its share price has generally trended upwards, how much debt the company has taken on (some debt is OK to pay for future expansion, for example, but too much is a worry) and whether or not the experts quoted in the business pages of the national newspapers or in specialist magazines such as the *Investors Chronicle* are also positive about the company you like.

If you've done all that and the share price in the company you've bought dips for no apparent reason, i.e. the fundamentals you've examined have not changed, then you should definitely hang on to your stock and maybe even take the opportunity to buy more while it's cheaper.

If on the other hand you find out that the managing director has been replaced by the post-room boy or one of the drugs your pharmaceutical company produces has been banned because it's putting hairs on the chests of women, then you should think about getting out quickly and then reassessing whether or not you still think it's a good buy.

It all seems a bit much for me

Well, if it does seem like a bit too much work, or if you don't have a lot of money to put away, you might be better off investing via a pooled fund rather than doing so directly.

In most cases individual shares are a worse buy for investors on a budget than for those with pots of cash to play with. The cost of dealing, even online, means that your chance of making any sort of profit is greatly reduced.

For those of you who want to invest only a set amount of money each month, say £50, it makes far more sense to put this into a collective fund, particularly a tracker.

The Jargonator: FTSE 100

The FTSE 100 – or the Footsie, as you'll sometimes see it written and hear it pronounced – has nothing to do with fondling your shares under the table while looking longingly into your fund manager's eyes. The FTSE 100 is an index that measures the performance of the shares of the one hundred largest companies listed on the London Stock Exchange. It measures the daily share price performance of those one hundred firms. If the FTSE 100 is up, it means there are more people buying than selling and share prices have risen. Conversely, if more people are dumping shares the index goes down. There are several other indices, such as the FTSE 250, and each one provides a quick snapshot as to whether people are making or losing money.

Bull versus bear market

A bull market is typified by generally rising stock prices, high economic growth and strong investor confidence. Bear markets are the opposite. They are characterised by falling stock prices, bad economic news and low investor confidence. To be bullish means you have an optimistic outlook. You are bearish when you believe a particular stock, sector or the overall market is about to fall.

A tracker? Isn't that a cereal bar?

Er, no. Funds can be split into two basic types: (1) active or managed funds, where the fund manager picks and chooses the shares he or she wants to invest in; and (2) passive funds that merely mirror or track the performance of a particular stock market index, such as the FTSE 100.

With managed funds, the guy running that fund (who may well have slicked-back hair and braces) buys shares in companies that he hopes will do better than a particular index. It is his job to pull in returns above and beyond the wider stock market but in doing so he often gets it wrong and invests in companies that suck.

In fact, studies have shown that over the long term nine out of ten managed funds fail to keep up with the index, with the average tracker fund beating 75% of managed funds. Of course there will always be some managed funds that do better than trackers – the problem is trying to identify them in advance.

Why do managed funds do so badly?

Trackers do better than most managed funds mainly because the charges on a tracker fund are much lower. They don't employ expensive fund managers who continually buy and sell shares and, unlike managed funds, they do not charge you upfront fees that can be as high as 5% of what you invest. What's more, a managed fund will charge you around 1.5% in annual management fees, whereas a tracker charges 1% or less.

That may not sound like much but, if you stuffed £1,000 into a tracker fund and £1,000 into a managed fund, and both returned 10% a year (a tidy sum), that would only translate to 7.5% for the managed fund, once you've factored in all your fees, and 9% for the tracker.

After ten years your managed fund would be worth £2,061 but your tracker would be worth £2,367 and over 25 years your tracker would have grown into a considerable £8,623 compared with £6,098 for the man in the pinstripe suit.

What makes share prices rise?

Five main things affect the price of your shares: (1) the economy, (2) company news, (3) analysts' reports, (4) press recommendations and (5) sentiment.

A **healthy economy** drives up company profits and, generally speaking, pushes the price of its shares higher. If the economy is weakening, however, company profits fall and share prices drop. 'The kind of information you need to pay close attention to is employment data, reports from the Bank of England's monetary committee to see where interest rates are heading, trade with other countries, retail sales and manufacturing reports,' says the London Stock Exchange (LSE).

When looking at economic data you need to think not only how the wider economy will be affected but also whether certain sectors will be more affected than others. A rise in interest rates, for example, is often a kick in the nuts for house builders and retailers, because people tend to borrow and spend less, but not so much of an issue for pharmaceutical companies.

Companies whose profits are closely tied to the health of the economy are known as cyclical stocks, while those not too affected, such as pharmaceutical firms, are called defensive stocks.

News coming out of a company also greatly influences its share price. If, for example, a company puts out a profits warning the price of its shares will droop as quickly as your ability to perform after a few too many pints. If, however, a director buys shares in the firm it may signal that the company's prospects are improving and its share price might rise.

Try to think laterally about the information you receive. If a competitor to a company you've bought shares in produces some fantastic gizmo, remember that this will probably have an adverse affect on your company. Also think about the impact it will have on its suppliers. An increase in sales of mobile phones with built-in cameras will not only be good for phone companies but will also be good for firms that supply the cameras. Similarly, if sales of this book rocket the number of chicken tikka jalfrezis sold by the Dulwich Tandoori will also go through the roof.

Reports produced by independent **analysts** also influence share prices. If an analyst changes his or her recommendation from buy to sell, the shares of the company he or she has analysed might rise.

'Remember, however, that a recommendation an analyst puts out will affect the share price very quickly and become irrelevant in hours,' says the LSE. 'This is because the analyst will usually say a stock is a buy within a particular price range. If the price moves above their target the shares may not be worth buying.'

But analysts' reports are always worth reading even if the recommendation is out of date, since they will contain useful information on how the company is doing and how its business is developing.

The financial pages of most national **newspapers** as well as investment **magazines** contain share tips and these, like analysts' reports, can have an effect on share prices. If a journalist recommends a share, the price will usually rise; if they write a negative story, the price will fall. Again, these moves happen very quickly, so, if you are going to follow a recommendation, you shouldn't wait around.

Finally, investor **sentiment** can greatly influence the price of equities but it can be impossible to predict and can be infuriating if, for example, you have bought shares in a company that you think is a good buy but the price remains flat.

> 'Investor sentiment can lead to irrational buying of shares, such as in the technology boom of the late 1990s, when investors paid extremely high prices for shares and ignored traditional valuation measures until they realised prices had risen too far and resulted in a three-year bear market in equities,' says the LSE.

Why would I bother with a managed fund?

Good question. Unless you can find the 25% of managed funds that outperform trackers, there's no point trying. But that doesn't mean that trackers are perfect. One of the biggest criticisms of a tracker, which follows an index such as the FTSE 100, is that your investments are not properly diversified.

For example, around 40% of the FTSE 100 is made up of banks and other financial shares. That means if the Fat Belly banks do badly the index would suffer and so too would your tracker fund.

A fund manager, meanwhile, might have seen this coming and switched out of a few of the banking shares and bought a few more pharmaceutical stocks instead.

Also, if you've found a sector that you're particularly keen on, such as the pharmaceutical sector, and you don't feel comfortable or have sufficient funds to buy shares directly, then investing in a fund that specialises in that area is your best bet.

Experts are adamant that a good fund manager can beat the market but being able to find those funds is difficult. To help you, it's best to speak to an independent financial adviser (IFA), who recommends – for a fee – funds run by all companies. A good place to start your IFA search is www.unbiased.co.uk. Choosing a tracker fund is much simpler: basically look for the one with the lowest charges.

So how do I buy a managed fund?

There are three ways to buy these funds, which can be structured as unit trusts or OEICs. First you can go direct to the fund manager but you will pay roughly 5% of the value of your investment in upfront charges as well as around 1.5% each year in management fees.

Second, you could use a fund supermarket, such as www.iii.co.uk or www.fundsnetwork.co.uk, which will rebate some of the upfront charge. Or, third, you could use a discount broker, such as www.hargreaveslansdown.co.uk or www.bestinvest.co.uk, which will rebate the entire upfront charge and some of the annual management fee.

Tips for choosing a managed fund

Consider past performance but remember it's not the be-all and end-all. Check the money pages of the weekend newspapers or visit www.funds-sp.com or www.morningstar.co.uk to get the lowdown on the past performances of various funds. Remember to look back as far as you can, or at least the last three to five years. Just because a fund did spectacularly well last year, it does not mean it won't do spectacularly badly next year.

Find out who's running the fund. Some portfolio managers stay with the same fund for years while others come and go. Before shoving your money into a well-performing fund, make sure that the manager currently in the driving seat was the one responsible for that growth. Also, check out how the manager fared during more turbulent years, since that's a good indicator of his or her worth.

Compare the fees of the fund you like and make sure you're not being ripped off. Yes, managed funds are more expensive than tracker funds but that doesn't mean you have to pay over the odds. If you're after a global equity fund, check the price of other global equity funds to give yourself peace of mind. Do not, however, choose one fund over another just because it is the cheapest – check the performance first.

Don't believe the hype. Fund managers trip over themselves to get you to part with your cash, so be sceptical about any promotional material or adverts you see in the press or online. Always read the small print to find out exactly what claims are and are not being made.

Nine questions to ask yourself before you invest in stock

1. Is it in a sector you think will do well?
2. What's the company's track record like?
3. Is the company growing?
4. Does the company offer something unique or does it have a lot of competition?
5. How much money does it have in the bank?
6. How volatile is its share price, i.e. how has it moved over the last three to five years?
7. Is it considered a high-growth, high-risk company or is it a stable, low-growth firm?
8. What sort of dividends does it pay out?
9. How do the press and other city analysts view the company?

Ten equity investing tips …

1. Use your ISA overcoat to wrap around your equity investments. It'll keep them safe from the taxman, leaving more money for you. You usually have to pay tax on all the profits you make from your investments, but an ISA allows you to put up to £7,000 (£7,200 from April 2008) away each year and pay no tax at all on the profits.
2. Decide why you want to invest in the stock market. Knowing your objectives is an essential starting point. Are you saving

generally for the future or to achieve an important life goal, such as buying a new home or sending your kids to university? As a rule of thumb, you shouldn't invest in the stock market for less than five years.

3. Figure out whether you want income, growth or a mixture of the two. Shareholders can generally aim to receive two types of return on their shares – growth as the share price increases and income in the form of dividends.

4. Determine your appetite for risk. If you want bigger returns from the stock market you'll have to take more risk. If you keep all your cash in a savings account you'll face virtually zero investment risk but your return will be lower and inflation could eat away at it. Age is also a factor: if you are younger, you may prefer to be more aggressive and take higher risks.

5. Reduce your risk by diversifying your portfolio. It is important to buy shares in different sectors and geographical regions. Some investors may prefer to do this through a collective fund, such as a tracker, a unit or an investment trust.

6. Decide what sort of service you want. If you want to invest directly and make all of the decisions yourself, you need a simple DIY execution-only account. Some execution-only stockbrokers also provide research on individual stocks to help with decision making.

7. Monitor your shares. Buying shares is just the beginning. As a rule you shouldn't pay too much attention to the daily fluctuations of share prices, but that doesn't mean you shouldn't keep an eye on the City pages of the national newspapers or your broker's research pages for news about your shares.

8. Invest your cash at regular intervals rather than in one go. Everyone knows that to make money from the stock market

you need to buy when the market is at its lowest and sell when it's at its highest. The trouble is, however, that no one knows when that is going to happen. Invest over time and you'll have more chance of hitting those sweet spots.

9. Know when to sell as well as when to buy. It's great news if the shares you've bought have done well. You have chosen well, stayed loyal to your investment and are reaping the benefits. But don't get greedy – remember that, until you sell up and the money is sitting safely in your bank, any profits you've made are just theoretical.

10. Think about adopting a stop-loss policy. This is where you automatically sell your shares if they fall by more than a certain amount, such as 15%. The theory is that, if the price of your shares falls below a certain limit, there must be a fundamental reason for it, and it's time to get out.

… and what not to do

- Don't invest on tips. Rumours are part and parcel of the stock market but one of the most common and costly mistakes you can make is to buy equities based on a hot tip from someone you barely know, such as your personal trainer, barber or takeaway-delivery guy, or worse still someone you know very well. These tips will lose you money and are as trustworthy as a politician on April Fools' Day.

- Don't sell up on a whim. Avoid getting caught up in day-to-day price swings. The long-term value of the shares you've bought are not reflected in short-term fluctuations. Unless the fundamentals of your investments change, hang on in there.

- Don't get emotionally attached to your shares. Remember, it's business, and business and pleasure don't mix. Think of your shares as fluffy little kittens or cute little puppies and you'll end up holding on to them for much longer than you should.

● Don't fall for the sales pitch. Any investment you make must be your own. It's dangerous to part with any money because you've fallen for the smooth patter of a salesman or -woman. The best brokers and investment advisers don't cold-call, so don't buy anything from someone offering a fantastic investment opportunity. You're likely to end up a loser.

The expert view: Choosing the right fund

Mark Taylor, director of savings, investments and pensions at Virgin Money

Short-term fluctuations in the stock market mean you need to take a long-term view, ideally at least ten years. Stock markets have performed well over the long term but you should not consider investing without preparing for the possibility of losing money, although, by investing sensibly and over the long term, this is unlikely to happen.

Unit-trust funds are one of the best ways to get started. These pool investors' money into a range of different companies, properties, gilts, bonds or cash – therefore spreading your risk. A unit trust is also managed by a fund manager, taking away the hassle of which stocks to choose.

There is a wide choice of funds available. Select a fund to get started that is right for you rather than what is currently being advertised. Establish a core holding such as a fund that invests in the UK or globally. Mindful that two-thirds of UK fund managers fail to beat the market over a three-year period, you may wish to consider an index tracker fund, which matches the performance of an index.

The ideal portfolio is a mix of cash, equities, property and fixed-interest securities such as bonds and gilts. The amount you hold in each of those asset classes will depend upon your attitude to risk. By holding a range of asset classes in your portfolio, you can reduce overall risk and improve potential returns. The right asset allocation is as important as picking the right fund, so you will need to review it every year and adjust accordingly. Alternatively, if you do not want or do not have time to monitor or adjust your portfolio, consider using a multimanager fund, which selects the 'best-in-breed' funds on your behalf, and how much to hold in each, taking a lot of the guesswork out of the equation.

Rather than trying to predict which way the stock market will go next, you should consider investing monthly rather than in one lump sum. This takes advantage of 'pound-cost averaging': basically your money buys more units when the market is down and less when it is on the way up, therefore evening out the risk of picking the wrong day to invest.

Most unit trusts are available as ISAs, so use your allowances to shelter any returns you make from income tax and capital-gains tax.

Finally, review how your portfolio is performing at least once a year. Fund managers are human and therefore prone to peaks and troughs in performance, so it's worth checking to see how they're doing in comparison with their peers.

Your place or mine: investing in property

Ever taken a sickie from work and had to watch daytime TV? Of course you have. Well, apart from all the ads about slipping over in the workplace and consolidating your loans into one easy-to-manage payment, you'll have also noticed the unbelievable array of property-development programmes.

These are usually programmes about how shoving an extra toilet under the stairs can increase the price of your pad; about how sellers should declutter their homes until they look like a doctor's waiting room; and about how you can flog your four-bed townhouse and use the money to buy a flat in the suburbs, a manor house in Bulgaria, a farmhouse in Lithuania and a castle in Estonia.

Basically, people have gone property mad. But it's little wonder. Since 1996, house prices in the UK have jumped up by 187% with the cost of an average house rising from around £62,000 to almost £180,000. To put that in perspective, shares went up by just 61% over the same period; our salaries increased by 54%; and the price of a Big Mac went up by 16%.

The upshot is that everybody is piling into property, either directly or through property investment funds, with house prices expected to grow by a further 8% by the beginning of 2008.

'Tight demand conditions reported by estate agents have not yet shown any signs of easing, and this will support house-price growth,' says the high-street building society Nationwide. 'On top of that, probably the biggest factor supporting the UK housing market is the lack of supply. The UK has a notoriously slow supply response and there are not enough new houses being built for the number of people who want to live in them.'

There you have it. People can't build houses quickly enough to match our insatiable demand for them. The thing about property is that everyone understands it. You have to do a lot of swotting up to understand exactly how equities or bonds work but property's easy – you buy a place, you do it up, you live in it or rent it out, and when you come to sell it's either gone up or down in value.

The problem, however, is that these TV programmes make it look as if everyone could make money from investing in property, when in fact it's getting harder and harder to squeeze out a profit.

Does that mean I should steer clear?

No, but it does mean you have to do your homework. Remember, there are a number of downsides to investing in property. For starters, it's much harder to liquidise compared with bonds or shares. And by liquidise I don't mean turning your flat into a banana-and-apricot smoothie but being able to sell it and recoup your cash. You can sell a share at any time, but you may have to wait up to twelve months or maybe longer to unload a house or flat.

What's more, property is a very high-maintenance investment. You can't just buy it and put it to the back of your mind like equities and bonds (although that's unwise, too). Your property investment will need constant updating and modernising. You will also need to cover ongoing costs such as council tax, mortgage payments, service charges and repair bills.

On top of that, property is also expensive to buy. You can pick up a share for just a few quid but any piece of real estate is likely to set you back at least six digits – any more than that and, unless you're a Russian billionaire, you might want to show the seller two digits of your own.

The purchase price is also not the only cost involved. There will be stamp duty to pay, lawyers, surveyors and agents to feed, removal costs, insurance costs and possibly renovation costs.

But that doesn't mean property doesn't have its upsides. First and foremost, it is much less vulnerable to intense market swings than any other type of investment. The value of property doesn't get completely wiped out, as it can for equities. While house prices can go down – and they do, you know, by more than 10% between 1989 and 1996 – there is always going to be some value in the land the property is built on.

You can also enjoy property in much more of a hands-on way (though not if you invest in property companies or an investment fund) than you can with equities and bonds. Not only can you see it, smell it and touch, it but you can also live in it and rent it out to friends and family.

But you need also to think carefully about it – the market is not as juicy as it once was.

Buy-to-let

A perfect example of how some of the juice has left property is in the buy-to-let market – the most common way for people to invest in property. As it says on the tin, buy-to-let is when you buy a flat or house and then let it out to give yourself a rental income. It's a very popular way to invest because you can not only make money from your tenants but you can also make money from any rise in property values.

Buy-to-let has been a real money spinner in the past but buy-to-let properties now account for 50% of all repossessions sold at auction, even though buy-to-let mortgages make up less than 10% of the total mortgage market.

The problem is that it has become much harder to make money from renting out your property. Not only because the increase in house prices has meant you have to borrow more to purchase your buy-to-let property, but also because interest rates have increased from 3.5% to 5.25% since 2003, making the cost of borrowing even higher.

'Higher house prices and interest rates mean the gross yields available on new buy-to-let purchases are less favourable than they were,' Nationwide told me. 'However, because of strong tenant demand, void periods (the time when your property might be empty) should be lower than in the past.'

So how do I make money from buy-to-let?

The first thing you need to do is some maths. Before deciding on a buy-to-let property, it is essential to work out the achievable rental yield to see whether it's worth the effort. Renting your place out for £2,000 a month or £24,000 a year might seem like a ton of money but, if the property you are renting out is worth £700,000 (the average price of a house in Kensington & Chelsea), you'll get back a disappointing yield of less than 3.4% (£24,000/£700,000) – much smaller than what you'd get if you stuffed your money in a Fat Belly bank account.

If the price of the property you are renting out is £360,000 (the price of the average house in Harpenden), however, and you are getting the same £2,000 a month, then the rental yield is 6.6% and well worth getting out of bed for.

But that assumes you haven't borrowed the money to buy your pad and happen to have £360,000 just lying around. To get a true reading of your profit you have to calculate the net property yield, which is the total rental income you get from your property minus the running costs divided by the current value, including the purchase costs.

So, if you get £24,000 a year in rent but pay £6,000 a year in mortgage costs and insurance and the value of your house is, say, £350,000 (after subtracting stamp duty and estate agency fees), then your net property yield is £18,000 – (£24,000 – £6,000)/£350,000 – which is 5.14%.

A decent return but the trouble is that the costs are far more extensive than most people realise and include:

- interest on money borrowed;
- insurance premiums – such as building and contents insurance;
- replacement of fixtures and furniture;
- servicing of electrical appliances;
- legal expenses;
- the costs of a letting agent if you choose to have one;
- ground rent and service charges (if you buy a leasehold property);
- redecoration;
- annual Corgi inspection of gas boilers and fires.

Not only that, but you'll have to pay income tax on any gains. If you are a cash buyer you'll still pull in a decent return despite all these costs, but if you're buying with a mortgage it's going to be touch-and-go as to whether you'll make a profit, and you may have to rely on your pad increasing in value to end up a big winner.

Nigel Terrington, chief executive of the specialist buy-to-let provider Paragon, is more optimistic. 'In terms of capital appreciation alone, the average buy-to-let investor has made over £7,700 this year [up until the start of 2007] just by owning a rental property. On top of that, he or she has generated almost £10,000 in rental income, an excellent total return on investment of £17,700 or 11.4% over the past twelve months. It was definitely a good year for most buy-to-let investors.'

Is it easy to borrow money and get involved?

Yes, as long as you have some money up front. The most common way to pay for a rental property is through a buy-to-let mortgage. Some Fat Belly banks and building societies will let you borrow up to 85% of the value of the pad you're after, though the majority will lend you only 75%, meaning you have to stump up 25% as a deposit.

How much they'll lend you depends on a combination of:

● **the gross rental income: Typically the amount of rent you get from your place needs to be at least 125 or 130% of your mortgage costs. That means if your mortgage is £1,000 a month you need to be pulling in £1,300 in rent.**

● **the value of the property: The Fat Belly banks will value the property independently and lend 75, 80 or 85% of the price they deem suitable.**

In addition, borrowers may also look at your earned income or a combination of your earned income and your rental income. So, if you're buying a place that can pull in a healthy amount of rent, it's relatively cheap to buy, you have a steady income and a deposit of around 20%, you shouldn't have any trouble. As with any mortgage, however, you need to make sure you shop around and check the best-buy tables to find the top deals.

But if I'm not making much profit what's the point?

It's true that after you've accounted for all the costs, including the cost of your mortgage, you might consider the profit you're collecting from rent to be nothing more than pocket money. But, if that pocket money comes in at £2,500 over the course of a year and you have four rental properties on the go, then that's a cool £10,000.

Indeed, the fact that projected rental income rather than salary levels are used to work out your level of borrowing means it's possible to build up an impressive property portfolio very quickly. After one buy-to-let property has been snapped up, you might release equity in that property, remortgage and buy more properties to let – a process that, to give it its posh name, is known as gearing.

Gearing?

Yes, gearing – the act of borrowing to increase returns. If you already have one property that has increased in value by 187% over the last ten years (as has been the case), it's possible for you to release some of that increase and put it down as a deposit on another buy-to-let property.

So, if you put down a deposit of £25,000, for example, on a £100,000 flat and it increases in value by £25,000 over a few years, the increase is 25%, yet your profit is 100% because your £25,000 deposit is now worth £50,000 if you sell.

But if property prices go the other way – which they are capable of doing – a 10% fall in prices would see your £25,000 investment turn to dust.

There are things, however, that you can try to do to avoid that.

Like what?

Most importantly, you need to make sure you buy a flat or house that isn't overvalued and is in an area with lots of potential tenants. But be open-minded – you might find that a two-double-bedroomed flat above a launderette, which is close to the Tube or a train station is cheaper and easier to rent out than a similar flat on a quieter tree-lined street fifteen minutes down the round. Likewise, a large five- or six-bedroomed house with a garden might be impossible to rent out in an area with lots of young professionals or families but could fly out of the door in a university town.

Also, if you are particularly interested in buying a place because you want to profit from an increase in property prices, you need to concentrate your efforts in an area with the most growth potential. Obviously it's impossible accurately to pick the next boom area but you can give it a go.

How?

Well, as always, past performance is a good place to start, although it should never be depended on. According to data from Halifax, the ten best-performing towns in the UK over the past ten years have been Newry in County Down (which has seen house prices increase by 371%), Walton-on-Thames in Surrey (368%), Seaham in County Durham (326%), Weybridge in Surrey (322%), Antrim in County Antrim (321%), Redruth in Cornwall (312%), Newham in London (307%), Hove in East Sussex (304%), Sevenoaks in Kent (303%) and Hackney in London (303%).

'Newry in Northern Ireland has seen house prices increase from £38,326 to £180,546 since 1996,' says Halifax. 'Two-thirds of towns have seen at least a £100,000 increase in their average house price over the same period. All of the 538 towns we looked at, bar Lochgelly in Fife and Greenock (which went up by £49,457 and £49,289), have seen at least a £50,000 increase in their average house price.'

Looking at winners from the past, however, may mean you've already missed the boat. But Prophit – an analysis organisation that publishes its data in *Your Mortgage* magazine and examines all the economic and demographic trends that drive property prices – has drawn up a list of towns in which it expects to see the greatest increases in house prices by 2010.

Newham is its number-one choice, with a predicted property increase of 43%. Thanet is next with rises of 38.3%, followed by the Isle of Wight with 33.9%, Hastings with 33% and Gosport with 32.2%. Also high on its list were Hackney, Haringey, Eastbourne, Ashford and Dover, with expected price rises of around 30%.

'Continued economic growth, rising employment and an ongoing lack of supply will continue to drive up house prices in the short term,' said that man again at Halifax. 'But higher interest rates, greater pressure on household finances and subdued real earnings growth will constrain housing demand.'

Seven ways to make buy-to-let work

1. **Buy the right property** – a very luxurious, expensive property is useless in a student town but would work nicely in a city centre.
2. **Refurbish your pad to a high standard.**
3. **Make sure you provide the sort of facilities that are suitable to your target audience.** If you are targeting young families, you need to buy a place with a garden, but if you're after young professionals think about installing a power shower, an Internet connection and a dishwasher.
4. **Present the property well for prospective tenants** – make sure it's clean and uncluttered.
5. **Vet any prospective tenants thoroughly** – a tenant with a poor history may wreck your investment.
6. **Keep your tenant happy.** If you don't respond quickly to their requests they might not pay you.
7. **Look after your property and maintain it as you would your own home**

Dangers of buy-to-let

Bad tenants: Finding and vetting new tenants can be the most difficult part of the buy-to-let experience. A bad tenant can seriously damage your investment, so either get a letting agent to find tenants for you, which may cost 10% of the monthly rent or a flat fee, or be prepared to check any potential tenant thoroughly yourself. Always check bank and employment references before handing over the keys and, if possible, try to rent to someone you, your friends, family or work colleagues are familiar with.

Location: Choose an area just because it's cheap and your property might remain as empty as the space behind Jade Goody's eyes. Choose an area with a growing working population, boosted by immigration, with low unemployment and rising incomes and you should be OK.

Empty property: Even if you choose your area wisely, you must be able to cope with the fact that it may remain empty for a while. According to the Association of Residential Letting Agents, the average void period is currently 26 days a year (26 in London, 30 in the northwest and 23 in the southwest). This needs to be factored into your calculations.

Tax: Remember (as if you could forget) that, when you sell your buy-to-let property, you will be taxed at between 20 and 40% on all relevant capital gains above a basic limit. Make sure you allow for this in your sums.

Overoptimism: House prices have increased by an incredible 187% over the past ten years, blitzing all the other asset classes. But that doesn't mean those rises will be repeated. Over the past thirty years prices have increased by a more modest 9% annually, according to Nationwide. Prices dropped by more than a tenth between 1989 and 1996 and could do so again, so be realistic about what you can achieve.

Real-estate investment trusts

If the thought of investing in the property market via the buy-to-let route sounds too expensive or risky, or you reckon it's just too much work, you might prefer to invest via a real-estate investment trust, or a REIT.

The beauty of a REIT is that it allows you to invest in both commercial property and residential property, which enables you to spread your investment risk much more widely than if you invested in a number of buy-to-let properties.

Commercial property, which includes shopping centres, office blocks and hotels, has performed particularly well over the last few years. In the past you had to invest in one of the big real-estate companies, such as Land Securities or British Land, to get an exposure. But that meant you were hit with double taxation. The company you invested in had to pay corporation tax on its property-related activities while you then had to pay income tax on dividends and capital gains as well.

But investing in a property company with a REIT structure avoids this. As long as the REIT you invest in pays out at least 90% of its profits to shareholders in the form of dividends, it doesn't have to pay corporation tax on its property-related activities, leaving you better off. Why? Because by not paying capital-gains or corporation tax the fund has money to share with you.

The introduction of REITs at the beginning of 2007 has seen a number of property companies convert to REIT status, including Land Securities and British Land. This has increased your number of investment options and a large number of investors have already pushed money into the sector. To find out more visit www.reita.com.

Property or a pension?

A crisis of confidence in pensions – maybe, as we saw, triggered by Robert Maxwell or bad advice to workers to leave perfectly good company schemes (see 'Pensions versus ISAs' on Page 145) – has pushed many people away from the market. At the same time, the housing market's fantastic gains – increases of 187% over the last ten years according to Halifax – have pulled many of those same people into property.

But is pinning your hopes on residential property instead of a pension a good idea? In a word, no. Buying a large home that you can trade down at retirement or selling up one or two of your buy-to-let investments is a highly risky strategy. Too many of your eggs are in one tiny basket.

House prices are doing well now, but who knows what's going to be happening in twenty, thirty or forty years' time. One thing people agree on is that much of the spike in property values is to do with a lack of supply, but the government has made a long-term commitment to increase the housing stock, while interest rates have been on the rise for the last four years – making mortgages increasingly expensive.

There are also tax implications. Yes, trading down to smaller property at retirement is a tax-efficient strategy, since the gains you make from selling your primary residence are usually tax-free. But investing in buy-to-let property does not have this advantage and any gains would be taxable up to a rate of 40%.

But that is not to say that property doesn't have its place. The perfect solution would be to invest in both a well-diversified pension and property. Don't forget that you can invest in the residential-property market via REITs, which you can in turn place in a SIPP (self-invested personal pension) to shield it from the taxman.

The name is Bond, investment Bond

Bonds, or fixed-income securities as they are also known, are a lot less hairy than equities, and those attracted to this asset class are much more interested in being gently stirred rather than shaken. Generally speaking, they are a safer bet. Bonds are less volatile than most types of shares but, unfortunately, that also means you're not going to make as much money from them over the long term.

According to figures from the investment bank Barclays Capital, £100 invested in UK government bonds in 1945 would be worth only £164 in today's money with the interest reinvested. The same amount stuffed into equities, however, would have turned into £4,000 if you had ploughed all your dividends back in.

But that shouldn't be surprising. Government bonds, also known as gilts, are almost risk-free, because you can be pretty certain the government will be around in five, ten or fifteen years' time to return the money you gave it. That sense of security, however, comes at a price: lower returns.

Corporate bonds, on the other hand, can be a much riskier prospect but pay out higher levels of interest. As a result, corporate bonds have been the best-performing asset class over the last ten years, according to those boys and girls at Barclays Capital, returning 8.1% a year – topping equities, which pulled in 5%, and kicking the amount you'd get from a Fat Belly bank (2.9%) to the kerb.

Over the much longer term, however, equities have always outperformed both government and corporate bonds. But that doesn't mean bonds should be ignored. They are a great way to diversify your portfolio and are a crucial asset class for those who've invested in riskier assets for many years and want to move that money into something safer to avoid losing what they've built up.

What exactly are bonds?

Basically, bonds are like IOUs, as we saw under 'What are my investment options?' on Page 124. You may want to go and take another look before reading on.

The income from them is known as the bond yield and is generally higher than the interest you'd get from a savings account because of the extra risks involved, the biggest being that the company you lend your money to goes bust and is not around in five years' time to pay you back.

So should I invest in bonds?

Well, yes and no. Bonds are basically a halfway house between saving your cash in a Fat Belly bank account and shoving it into equities.

They are a good diversifier, because they tend to perform differently from shares. For example, when stock markets fell between 2000 and 2002 and central banks cut interest rates to kick some life back into the economy, the price of bonds increased – helping investors to offset some of their equity losses.

But when interest rates are rising, as they are as I write (rates have increased by around 2 percentage points since 2003), it's not such a great time to invest in fixed-income securities because their value is likely to fall.

In fact, during the twelve months leading up to the start of 2007 only three of the 94 corporate-bond funds available on the market made money, according to the rating agency Standard & Poor's. What's more, if you'd put £1,000 into the largest of the 94 funds, the Halifax corporate-bond fund, which has almost £4 billion invested in it, you'd have got back £7 less than what you'd put in.

But I thought interest-rate rises were a good thing

If we're going to continue on the James Bond theme, then rising interest rates are a bit like that guy with the white cat. You know, the one with the dodgy eye and no hair – Blo-something or other. Anyway, rising interest rates are an archenemy of the bond investor.

First, you need to remember that when you invest in bonds you are effectively lending your money to the company issuing the bond, which means they are effectively borrowing money from you. Now we all know that if interest rates rise the cost of borrowing goes up – the Fat Belly banks increase their overdraft rates, credit-card companies add a few more digits to their APRs and mortgage providers push up the price of their loans.

The same is true in the bond market. Lenders, let's call them you, demand a higher rate of return on the money you dish out, which increases the cost of borrowing for bond issuers. The problem is that, if you invest in the riskier end of the market, such as in junk bonds (see the Jargonator on Page 184), this increase could financially cripple some companies. Paying out a higher rate of interest on all the money they've borrowed could send them over the edge – meaning you might not get some or any of the interest promised to you or, worse still, lose all the money you invested.

Is that all I need to worry about?

I'm afraid not. The interest you get from bonds is fixed, so, if interest rates rise and the returns on newly issued bonds, savings accounts and other investment products increase, the rate you're getting from your bond looks comparatively rubbish.

The problem is that, when you come to sell your bond, which you can do at any time, even though it may have a life of one, five, ten or fifteen years, its price may have fallen and you could get back less than what you invested.

You what?

Well, imagine I had a chicken that laid five eggs a month and you had a lazy one that laid only four eggs a month. OK, now if we both sold our chickens at the local chicken market, including details of their egg-laying prowess, my five-a-month bionic chicken would fetch a higher price than your lesser specimen.

The same is true of bonds. If I have a bond that pays 5% a year and you have one that pays 4% a year, my bond would command a higher price if I sold it on the stock market.

Let's apply that same logic: if the Bank of England reduces interest rates from 5 to 4% but your bond continues to pay out a fixed rate of 5%, it would sell for more because it lays more eggs than everybody else's.

Consequently, the very best time to buy bonds is when interest rates have peaked and look as if they're about to tumble, such as between February 2000 and July 2003, when interest rates fell from 6% to 3.5%.

Are interest rates the only thing that affects bond prices?

No. Interest-rate changes are the key determinant but other factors have an influence. Corporate-bond prices, for instance, will also be affected by the general health of the issuing company, while government-bond prices can be affected by the government's behaviour. For example, if it has a rising deficit, which means it's spending more than it's earning through taxation, then it suggests to the market that it might start issuing more bonds. And the more government bonds (or anything for that matter) that come on to the market, the cheaper they become.

The performance of the stock market also has an influence. If share prices are falling across the board, people tend to switch out of equities and move their money into bonds because it is viewed as a safer and more stable investment. This extra demand pushes up prices.

Also, if a company's or a government's credit rating gets downgraded by one of the rating agencies, such as Moody's or Standard & Poor's, the price of its bond drops. A downgrade, indicating that an issuer is less likely to repay its debt, is bad news for the issuing company, while an upgrade makes them happy.

Rating agencies? Downgrades? What are you on about?

Well, one way of working out how risky a bond is is via its credit rating. These ratings are supplied by a number of credit-rating agencies, of which the best known are Standard & Poor's and Moody's. The idea is that the higher the credit rating given by Standard & Poor's or Moody's, the less likely that company is to have problems paying you back.

Investors are therefore prepared to accept a lower rate of interest for bonds with high credit ratings because the risk that that company will default, the posh word for not paying you interest or returning your cash to you, is much lower.

Credit-rating agencies review their ratings on a regular basis and may upgrade or downgrade a company's rating if they think its financial health has improved or declined.

With triple-A-rated bonds, the highest-ranking bonds, the risk of default is quite small and Moody's estimates that fewer than 1% of triple-A-rated bonds will default over the following ten years. With triple-B-rated bonds, that risk of default rises to almost 5%, while B-rated bonds have an almost one-in-two chance of default.

So where do I buy bonds?

You can buy gilts through the post office or a stockbroker. Corporate bonds can be bought only via a stockbroker. If you don't want to buy bonds directly, you can choose from a variety of bond funds run by investment companies, which pool your money together with that of other investors.

Bond funds will invest in dozens or perhaps hundreds of different bonds to minimise the risk that an individual bond will default. They invest in different regions, such as the UK or Europe, and usually invest in only one of the three main types of bonds, namely government, corporate and high-yield.

The key thing to remember with bond funds is that the higher the rate of income they offer, the riskier their portfolio of investments will be. A higher rate does not mean that one bond fund is better than another.

Before going for one particular fund over another, always compare its fees with a similar type of fund to make sure you're not being ripped off. So, if you're after a corporate-bond fund, check the price of other corporate-bond funds to give yourself peace of mind.

Running yield versus redemption yield

When choosing a bond fund, make sure you know the difference between what's called the running yield and what's called the redemption yield. The running yield tells how much income you're getting on the current value of investment, while the redemption yield more importantly tells you the overall return you can expect to make when the individual bonds within the fund mature. The redemption yield is also a better gauge, because it takes into account any annual fees your manager may charge.

And how much should I invest?

Many people argue that you should always invest some of your portfolio in bonds so that you're protected against the volatility of shares. One rule of thumb widely used is that you should go for the same percentage as your age. So, if you're thirty, you should have 30% of all your investments in bonds, while forty-year-olds should have at least 40%. But these are

>>

just crude guidelines and it really depends on your individual attitude to risk.

During periods of high stock market volatility you might want to increase the amount you shove into bonds, but it's important to remember that over the long term bonds have never performed as well as equities.

The Jargonator: Junk bonds

Junk bonds, also known as high-yield bonds, are issued by companies that carry a speculative credit rating. Speculative-grade issuers usually have questionable track records, or have experienced significant events that undermine their ability to pay interest and the money they borrowed.

What else can I do with my money?

Well, if what we've looked at so far is too boring for you, you might want to consider investing your money in some of the more exotic asset classes. And by exotic I don't mean shoving your cash into Bermudan bonds, Egyptian equities or Paraguayan property. I'm talking about sticking your hard-earned cash into wine, art or stamps.

Are you having me on?

No, but before we look more closely at these investment opportunities let's get a few things straight. For starters, wine, art and stamps should never make up more than 10% of what you're planning to invest. Second, these assets, unlike equities, bonds and property, are not regulated by the investment watchdog the Financial Services Authority and are consequently fraught with danger. Third, your minimum investment is likely to be much higher than it is with mainstream investments. And, last, there are no regular dividends or interest to rely on.

Basically, these alternative asset classes are much riskier investment options, but that doesn't mean they should be written off. They have useful diversification properties and, despite sounding a little bit Mickey Mouse, there is a chance you could make some serious money from them.

If you already have a strong interest in art, for example, investing in it is a great way to use your expertise to make you money. If, however, you think Monet is what the French use to buy baguettes with, you're better off investing your time learning about equities or bonds. And just because you've drunk a lot of wine, it doesn't make you an investment expert.

Wine: a corker of an investment

That crown would most definitely go to wine. It is the most popular and developed of the alternative assets and is what we will concentrate on the most.

Statistics show that since the early 1980s the price of the top wine vintages has increased by more than the FTSE 100. Indeed, wine-investment expert Premier Cru claims that between January 1990 and January 2007 wine indices increased by almost 15% a year on average – more than double the FTSE All-Share. What's more, figures from the London International Vintners Exchange (Liv-ex) show that in 2006 its benchmark index – the Liv-ex 100 – rose by almost 50%, its highest increase in ten years.

So credible has fine wine become as an asset class that the Treasury said it was going to allow it to be held within a self-invested personal pension or a SIPP, as it's more commonly known. The fact this never actually happened makes sense – wine is probably too risky to be relied on to finance your retirement – but the fact that it was considered shows just how far the asset class has come.

So do I just walk into Thresher's to get my portfolio started?
No. You're not going to get rich buying a Bulgarian red for £3.99. Wine merchants recommend an absolute minimum investment of £10,000 in order to establish a good, balanced wine portfolio.

It is possible to invest less but key to making money in this area is buying quality over quantity. For example, if you've got £1,000 to spare buy two £500 cases of wine rather than five priced at £200.

And they are?

Well, just as your first foray into shares is likely to be in a FTSE 100 company, your first wine investment should be in Bordeaux. As a rule of thumb, the premium wines from the best vintage will provide the best returns – typically the top thirty châteaux in Bordeaux.

For example, the 1990 Château Latour from Bordeaux released the following year by wine merchant Berry Brothers & Rudd at just over £400 for a twelve-bottle case would now go for close to £3,000 a case.

Since 1855, Bordeaux wines have been classified into five ranks and the crème de la crème are called the first growths, which take fifteen to twenty years to mature. The better the wine the longer it takes to get to maturity – like shares, wine is a long-term investment.

Buying from a proven vintage is a good bet with 1986 being one year picked out for praise. Generally speaking, any wine from a good vintage is better than a good name from a poor year – never assume that a particular winemaker will always provide good returns.

How do I buy these vintages?

No house in the world will sell to you directly, so you have to buy through a merchant. However, the market is unregulated and is inhabited by a number of dodgy traders. If, for example, you decide to buy your wine *en primeur*, which means you buy the wine before it's been bottled and is still in the cask, you need to be certain your merchant will still be afloat in two years' time when you come to take delivery of your wine.

The independent website www.investdrinks.org lists some of the companies that fall foul of Department of Trade and Industry regulations, so make sure you check it out before parting with any money. Choosing one of the most visible and well-known merchants, however, should stand you in good stead.

What else do I need to know?

Well, something that'll make you particularly happy is that any profits you make on your wine investment are free of capital-gains tax. Because the Inland Revenue views wine as a 'wasting chattel' – an old tax term used to describe something that deteriorates in value – you're able to keep all your profits.

Also, unless you're planning to drink your wine, which is highly inadvisable for an investor, store your wine within a bonded warehouse controlled by HM Customs & Excise. If you don't do that you'll be hit with an import fee for each case of wine you buy plus 17.5% VAT on the purchase price. Having your wine stored in a bonded warehouse also guarantees that the conditions inside will be perfect for the life of your wine.

Remember, knowing what a fair price is for a particular wine is crucial when making an investment, since prices can vary widely. Current prices can be checked by signing up to auction catalogues or specialist magazines, such as *Decanter*, or by scouring websites, such as www.winesearcher.com.

If you don't know much about wine or you're not interested in learning, ask for expert advice from a specialist broker. Your broker should not charge you a consultation or buying fee but will take 10% commission when you come to sell.

Seven tipple tips

1. **Deal only with reputable merchants but make sure you shop around for advice and prices.**
2. **Buy in bond so you don't have to pay excise duty and VAT upfront.**
3. **Buy sealed cases in original boxes – they'll be worth more.**
4. **As with equities be prepared to invest for the long term.**
5. **Insure your wine for its market price rather than the price you paid.**

6. **Don't blindly just buy the big names – they may have less profit potential.**
7. **Buy a small number of quality wines rather than spreading your investments too thinly.**

Art: an investment masterpiece?

Company accounting scandals or terrorist attacks don't affect the price of art, as they can other forms of investment. In fact, when people's confidence in the economy declines the price of art increases – making it a good diversifier.

What's more, while share certificates are filed away in a dusty box or tucked away in the same drawer as your pants and socks, you can stick your art investment over the fireplace and not only watch it possibly increase in value over a number of years but also get a lot of pleasure from it.

The problem with this tangible asset is that, although it's possible to make money from your investment, not many people do. Art's investment performance has been pretty unspectacular over the years making it an unsuitable place to stick the bulk (or arguably any) of your cash.

To increase your chances of making any money you need to make sure you invest for the long term and buy only those pieces that make a strong impression on you. Not only does that hopefully mean your view will be shared by other buyers when you come to sell, but at least you would have got some value out of it if your investment depreciates.

Remember, if you're buying at auction, you'll also need to include the auction house's commission, which isn't included in the hammer price. At Sotheby's, for example, there is a buyer's premium of 20% on pieces up to £10,000, 15% up to £50,000 and 10% above that.

Unless you're very interested in art and are in the privileged position of not having to rely on your investment, you should probably steer clear. You're better off investing your time and money in the mainstream asset classes. Yes, people do make money from art but a lot more make money from equities.

Six artistic tips

- Find out how much other works have gone for in recent sales to work out how much money you should part with.
- Remember, you don't have to buy only at auction houses. For smaller investments, websites such as www.britart.com sell pieces from around £100 a pop.
- Check the condition of the piece even if only with the naked eye to be sure it is in good order – be aware of flaking paint and faded colours.
- In the same way the Darth Vader figure I've had since I was ten is worth more today in its original packaging, you should try to keep the original frame for your piece wherever possible. If you can't, try to get hold of a period frame and be aware that modern reproductions, even the very best, can lower the value of the painting.
- Paintings and photos do not like direct sunlight. So keep your pieces properly protected from harmful elements.
- Before parting with your cash, visit an auction house without your wallet to familiarise yourself with how the whole process works. Don't run before you can walk.

Stamps: do they lick other investments?

There are close to 50 million stamp collectors worldwide and stamps are the third most popular sales category on eBay, the mother of all Internet auction sites. What's more, the investment bank Salomon Brothers says stamps were one of the top four investments of the twentieth century, pulling in an average return of 10% a year.

According to the London-based stamp firm Stanley Gibbons, which offers a number of investment funds, some rare stamps have increased in price by more than 400% over the last five years. Again, the minimum investments in this area are high, but £5,000 gets you a guaranteed return of 4% a year for a three-year investment while a ten-year deal gets you 6%.

You need to bear in mind that it can take many years for your stamp investment to pay off, but for those of you thinking seriously about investing in this area Stanley Gibbons's website www.stanleygibbons.com is a good place to start.

PART 4:
AND NOT
FORGETTING...

Taxation: it needn't be taxing

There are three certainties in life: death, the fact that a James Bond film will be on TV over Christmas and taxes. But, while it's impossible to dodge your tax bill completely, there are many ways to reduce it.

For as long as tax has existed, people have been trying to get round it. For example, when window tax was introduced in 1669 on houses with more than ten windows, people immediately started blocking them up or trying to camouflage them.

Luckily, you don't have to do anything as drastic as sitting in the dark to escape the taxman, but reports suggest that you should be doing more than you currently are. Indeed, figures from IFA Promotion, the industry body responsible for promoting independent financial advice, show that around 80 per cent of us pay more tax than we need to. In fact, the total amount we overpay in tax each year comes in at a mighty £8 billion or so, or around £300 for every UK household.

Now I'm not suggesting you do anything illegal to avoid the taxman's reach – this, after all, is about tax efficiency not tax avoidance – but just that you make sure you're not giving him more than you're legally required to. As Mark Twain once said, 'The only difference between a taxman and a taxidermist is that the taxidermist leaves the skin.'

So where do I start?

The first thing you need to do is make sure you're using all the investment tax breaks you're entitled to. For starters, if you're investing for your retirement, make sure you're doing it through a pension fund rather than anything else.

The tax relief you get on a pension makes it a no-brainer for basic-rate taxpayers and, especially, higher-rate taxpayers wanting to save for their retirement. The reasoning is simple: a basic-rate taxpayer, who pays income tax at 22% (falling to 20% from April 2008), has to pay only £78 into a pension to get £100 worth of investment, while a higher-rate taxpayer has to cough up only £60 to get the same £100 worth of investment.

Not only that, but the money you invest in a pension plan grows free of any income or capital-gains tax, and it's only when you draw an income from your pension at retirement that the Inland Revenue turns up to spoil the party, by which time you may well have slipped into a lower tax bracket, anyway.

Also, you should be able to take up to 25% of the money you invested in your pension as a tax-free lump sum.

ISA from your elbow

Next, make sure you use your annual ISA allowance. ISAs, short for individual savings accounts, are a tax-free way both to save and to invest your money. They are not a savings product in themselves, like a postal account or a global equity fund, but a kind of overcoat that you can wrap around the shoulders of your money to shield it from the taxman – a bit like Harry Potter's invisible cloak.

Without an ISA, you would have to pay tax on all the profits you make from your investments. But by investing up to £3,000 (rising to £3,600 from April 2008) a year in a cash ISA, or up to £7,200 a year in a stocks-and-shares ISA (as long as you haven't used your cash ISA allowance), you pay no tax at all on the profits.

National Savings

There are other tax-efficient savings plans for you to explore. NS&I, the government outfit that raises money for public spending by providing a range of savings and investment products, offers inflation-linked and fixed-interest savings certificates, premium bonds and children's bonds – all of which offer tax-free interest.

National Savings Certificates, first launched in 1916 (see Page 112), allow you to invest anything from £100 up to £15,000 tax-free, while putting as little as £100 or as much as £30,000 into Premium Bonds could net you a tax-free cash prize of £1 million.

Similarly, friendly-society savings schemes (see Page 119) offer tax incentives as long as you contribute no more than £25 a month or £270 as a yearly lump-sum payment. You do, however, need to keep your money invested for at least ten years to qualify for tax-free payments, while charges for these sorts of product can be high.

Exercise your capital-gains tax allowance

We all get a capital-gains tax (CGT) allowance of roughly £9,000 a year and so, if you want to sell a large amount of your investments and reckon you might exceed your CGT threshold in one year, you should think about selling up across two tax periods. Selling some of your investments in March, for example, and some just a few weeks later in April, which is the start of the new tax year, could save you a fortune.

But be warned: if you've sold shares you cannot buy them within the following thirty days, otherwise your CGT allowance becomes defunct. You can, however, buy them back straight away through an ISA as long as you haven't already used up your annual limit.

It also makes sense, purely from a tax point of view, to hold your investments jointly with someone else. Usually this will be your spouse or your partner, but it doesn't have to be – it can be anyone you choose. Since you both have the same CGT allowance of around £9,000 a year you can pocket gains of up to £18,000 before being robbed by the taxman.

Dying to pay tax?

Given that the only two certainties in life (apart from James Bond at Christmas) are death and taxes, it is rather ironic that the Inland Revenue clobbers you for tax after you've popped it as well.

Inheritance tax or IHT, as it's also known, stands at 40% and is levied on the value of almost everything you own over £300,000 (rising to £350,000 by April 2010). That may sound like a lot, and you may think you'll never exceed that limit, but a decade of rising house prices – which has seen property values increase by almost 190 per cent – has pushed millions of people into the IHT bracket.

Despite this, research from bank Bradford & Bingley shows that only one in fifty people who thinks he or she will be liable to pay IHT has taken steps to do something about it, while almost 50 per cent of us have no clue what the IHT threshold is.

Let's take a simple example. Imagine Mr Deadandburied has an estate (that's total wealth, not a car with a big boot) worth £350,000, which includes the value of his property, savings and investments, cars, jewellery and furnishings. His current IHT liability is £365,000 minus £300,000, or £65,000 and, because IHT is levied at 40%, Mr Deadandburied owes £26,000 to the laughing boys down at the tax office.

So how do I avoid HRT or IHT or whatever it is?

One thing you can do is make gifts while you are alive. Each year you can give away up to £3,000 tax-free to your kids, the postman or your mate down the pub free of IHT as long as you live for seven years after you've handed out your dosh.

What's more, any unused exemption from the previous tax year can be carried forward to the current year, which means you and your partner could gift assets worth £12,000 in one year.

You're also able to gift up to £250 to any number of people each tax year free of IHT and can additionally dish out up to £5,000 to the fruit of your loins as a wedding present or up to £2,500 to your grandchildren as a wedding gift. If you're feeling particularly generous, you can also give up to £1,000 to your mate Clive down the pub or anyone else who's getting married.

Another way to keep the taxman's clammy little hands off your estate is to make IHT-exempt gifts to charities, either during your lifetime or via your will. It is common for people with no surviving dependants to leave their entire estate to good causes, but that's not surprising – leaving your money to either the Inland Revenue or a charity is not such a hard decision to make.

Making a will should be your first step to ensuring your estate is shared out exactly as you want it to be. In case you don't, there are rules for divvying it out – called the law of intestacy – which could see your money going to family members who don't need it, for example, with your unmarried partner receiving nothing at all. By the way, if you leave everything to your spouse or civil partner, there's no inheritance tax to pay because they are classed as an exempt beneficiary.

Stamp out stamp duty

Every time you buy shares in a UK company you have to a pay 0.5% in stamp duty. Although 0.5% may not seem like much, it can quickly add up if you make the mistake of trading frequently.

So how do you get round stamp duty? Easy: hold your shares for the long term instead of constantly trying to beat the market on a short-term basis. Remember, investing in the stock market is a marathon, not a sprint.

Don't sell up your holdings on a whim. The long-term values of the shares you've bought are not reflected by short-term fluctuations. Unless the fundamentals of your investments change, hang on to them. Not only should this pay off in the long run, it will also save you a heap in stamp-duty charges.

Use your personal allowances

If you don't earn enough to pay tax, fill out an R85 form in order to stop 20% savings tax being deducted at source – it's estimated that non-taxpayers lose more than £300 million a year by not doing this. Also, if you're married or in a same-sex civil partnership, you can reduce your overall tax bill as a couple by switching savings to the non-taxpaying half of the relationship.

Similarly, if you're a higher-rate taxpayer – meaning you pay 40% on your savings interest – and your spouse is a lower-rate taxpayer, transfer your savings into your spouse's name, as long as you can trust her not to blow it all on shoes or him not to invest it all in beer. On pretax interest of £1,000 you would save yourself £200 a year.

Use gift aid when donating to charity

If you give to charity and you want to keep even more of your money out of the taxman's hands, you should do so via Gift Aid. Using Gift Aid means that every pound you donate turns into £1.28 for the charity because of tax relief. What's more, if you're a higher-rate taxpayer, you can reclaim a further 23p via your tax return so that every £1.28 donated costs you a mere 77p.

Claim your tax credits

There is more than £3 billion in unclaimed tax credits, including child tax credit, working tax credit and pension credit, floating around, according to those boys at IFA Promotion. Nine out of ten families are eligible for some sort of contribution, so make sure you know what you're entitled to and claw back some of what you've paid out in tax as benefits. Don't be shy – you've earned it.

Child trust funds

Another tax-free way to save money is through a child trust fund (see Page 115). The government will give you a £250 voucher to start your child's fund when it's born and will add another £250 to the fund when your child reaches the age of seven. You, your friends and your relatives are then free to add a further combined sum of £1,200 a year into your child's fund, all of which is tax-free. Remember, however, any wonga you tuck away in a CTF belongs not to you but to your kid, so if you can't trust the child you're funding forget it.

Get a room …

… or rent one, rather. If you've got a spare room in your house or flat, you might want to think about renting it out to a mate or a colleague from work. If you do, the Rent-a-Room scheme will allow you to receive rent of up to £4,250 a year free of tax. The scheme applies to a property only if it's your main residence. The only downfall is the toenails you might find in the sink.

Looking after the unexpected: buying insurance

Nobody likes thinking about the worst-case scenario, but unfortunately, when it comes to insurance, that's what you've got to do. If you've got a house, be mindful that it might burn down; if you've got a job, be aware that you might get sacked; and, if you've got a life (and I know you have), remember that you might lose it.

The problem with insurance is that it's easy to get ripped off and it seems that, if you do anything financial, such as take out a loan, apply for a mortgage or open a credit card, there are people trying to sell you insurance products at every turn.

In a lot of cases loading up on insurance is a total waste of time. I mean, why would you want credit-card insurance when the Banking Code already protects you against fraudulent use? And, if you're taking out a loan, why would you bother buying insurance that protects the lender rather than you?

But don't let these Mickey Mouse policies tarnish your view about insurance. If you've got kids and – like Starsky, Dempsey or Cagney – you have a partner who depends on you, then you need to take out some life insurance. It's not a scam.

If you don't have kids or someone who relies on your income, fine – you don't need to bother with life insurance. Also, if you're in a company pension scheme, you're probably already covered as far as life insurance goes. But if you're not, and anyone in your family would suffer financially if you weren't around, then it's vital you put some sort of safety net in place. The only time life cover is worth *not* considering is if you have no dependants at all. If you do, get considering.

But won't it cost me an arm and a leg?

No. A nonsmoking man aged 35 wanting £100,000 of cover for 25 years would pay less than £8 a month for life insurance, while a woman would pay less than £7 a month. When you consider that a packet of twenty cigarettes would set you back far more than a fiver, and two pints of beer and a packet of nuts would hit you for £7, it's not bad going.

Five things to avoid when buying life insurance

1. **Lying: Lie to your life insurer or fail to tell it crucial information about your health in order to lower your premiums and you might as well not bother buying a policy at all. Holding back information about your medical history, your current state of health or your drinking or smoking habits is known as nondisclosure. And this means your insurer may have the right to give you a great big bag of nothing when you die.**

2. **Salesmen: If you want to buy life insurance, don't do it at your local high-street bank or building society or you'll end up paying through the nose for it. Visit an independent financial adviser to get help finding the right policy, not a salesperson at a Fat Belly bank.**

3. **Overinsuring: If you earn the average wage of £25,000, there's no point buying a policy that pays out £1 million when you snuff it – you'll end up paying a fortune in premiums. As a rule, ten times your gross salary is enough for most people. Alternatively, buy enough insurance to cover any debts and provide up to around £150,000 for each of your kiddiewinks. So, if you've got a mortgage of £50,000 and one child, insure yourself for £200,000.**

4. **Choosing the wrong policy:** There are a number of different variations of life insurance ranging from a policy that covers a mortgage to one that pays out a tax-free monthly income instead of a lump sum. Make sure you buy one that suits your needs the most.

5. **Paying unnecessary tax:** The greedy taxman can take 40% of your estate above your inheritance tax (IHT) threshold of £300,000 (rising to £350,000 by April 2010). To dodge this whopping charge, put your life-insurance policy into trust – you not only avoid IHT but your beneficiaries will get their money more quickly.

One to avoid

Extended warranties: If something you've bought is going to break, statistics show it's going to do so in the first year. The good news is that if this happens you're covered by the manufacturer's guarantee, so forget about buying further cover. What's more, the Sale of Goods Act, which states that items must be of a decent quality and fit for their purpose, means that if an appliance goes wrong before you might expect it to then the place you bought it is liable to repair it regardless of whether the manufacturer's guarantee has run out or not.

Protect your income

Apart from life insurance, the other key cover you should seriously consider buying is income protection, particularly if you're self-employed.

Income-protection insurance is designed to pay out for whatever reason you might be unable to work and differs from critical-illness insurance in that it not only pays out a steady income rather than a straight lump sum, but it is also not dependent on your contracting one of a specified list of diseases.

As with all types of insurance, it's crucial you buy the exact type of income protection you need. There are three main definitions of not being able to work: being unable to do your job; being unable to do your job or a similar one you're qualified to do; and being unable to do any kind of paid work.

You need to decide whether you'd be up for doing another, perhaps less satisfying, job if you weren't able to do your one. If that's the case, then the cost of your cover will be cheaper. Buying protection to insure you against not being able to do just your current job, however, will cost you more.

You can also reduce the size of your premiums by buying a policy that makes you wait possibly sixty or ninety days for your first payout. The longer you can afford to go without your first payment, the cheaper your premiums will be.

If you're not self-employed and work for a company, check your contact to see whether or not your employer pays you if you're off sick for a certain period of time. If they do, then there's no need to worry about income protection.

INDEX